A *WESTERN HORSEMAN* BOOK

# Ride Smart

D1546967

---

*Improve Your Horsemanship Skills
on the Ground and in the Saddle*

---

## By Craig Cameron
### With Kathy Swan

Edited by Cathy Martindale
Photography by John Brasseaux

Illustrations by Ron Bonge

# Ride Smart

*Published by*
**WESTERN HORSEMAN** magazine

3850 North Nevada Ave.
Box 7980
Colorado Springs, CO 80933-7980

www.westernhorseman.com

*Design, Typography and Production*
**Western Horseman**
Colorado Springs, Colorado

*Cover photograph by*
**John Brasseaux**

*Printing*
**Branch Smith**
Fort Worth, Texas

*©2004 by Western Horseman*
*a registered trademark of*

**Morris Communications Corporation**
725 Broad Street
Augusta, GA 30901

*Second Printing: January 2005*

ISBN 0-911647-66-X

# DEDICATION

I've been blessed to have so many supportive people in my life who've taught me the real meaning of friendship and that success is not a place, but a direction.

To my family for instilling in me the conviction to pursue my dreams,

To my wife, Dalene, whose tireless and unselfish ways, support and sacrifice are the truest expression of love,

And to the magnificent animal we call the horse, who always keeps me honest and humble, I dedicate this book.

# ACKNOWLEDGEMENTS

There are many people to whom I'm very grateful and owe special thanks for their friendship, extraordinary support, guidance and never-ending encouragement.

| | | |
|---|---|---|
| Doug & Patsy Adams | Bill Glaspy | Barry & Arlene Moffit |
| Josh Allen | Bubba Goudeau | Butch & Joy Murray |
| Tom Bagby | Dr. Charles Graham | Ty Murray |
| Dr. & Mrs. Bruce Cameron | Cole Cameron Graybill | Homer & Mickey Owen |
| Bruce Cameron, Jr. | Darren Graybill | John Ross |
| Doug Cameron | David Graybill | Butch Royer |
| Johnny Cantu | C. P. Hamer | Jim Sanders |
| Marsha Chestnut | Frank Hamer | Bobby Steiner |
| Alvin Davis | Harrison Hamer | Red Steagall |
| Dennis & Jan Dodson | R. W. Hampton | Rick & Kathy Swan |
| Frances Franz | Charmayne James | Gary James Tidwell |
| Brendan Garrison | Ron & Brenda Massingill | Jeremiah Watt |
| Mark & Marlene Garrison | Bruce McShan | *Western Horseman* |

Thanks to great horsemen, past and present, for whom I have tremendous admiration and respect.

| | | |
|---|---|---|
| Keith Barnett | Tom Dorrance | Bill Kelly |
| Mark Chestnut | Al Dunning | Pat Patterson |
| Jimmy Cooper | Monte Foreman | Greg Ward |
| Tuffy Cooper | Bobby Hunt | Buster Welch |
| Jerry & Pepe Diaz | Ray Hunt | John White |
| Don Dodge | Bobby Ingersol | Jimmy Williams |

Thanks to Kathy Swan for her contribution of talent, knowledge, enthusiasm and unwavering perseverance to make this book as good as it could be.

And thanks to John Brasseaux for his artistic skill and tenaciousness in settling for nothing less than the perfect picture.

—*Craig Cameron*

# PREFACE

I first met Craig Cameron in the early 1990s at a ranch rodeo in Grand Junction, Colo., where I watched him work his magic on a couple of unstarted colts during the event's horsemanship demonstration. I've since been able to attend many more demonstrations and clinics, and, even better after all these years, I can now call him a close friend.

Craig has a way with people and horses. He's the kind of person who lights up a room the minute he walks in and the kind horses respond to easily. I was honored when he asked me to write his book. I wondered, though, if it was possible to harness his personality, not to mention his knowledge, and put it on paper. Creating a reader-friendly yet comprehensive manuscript is never an easy task, but Craig made it as easy on me as he makes things easy for horses.

When we developed the structure of this book, Craig wanted it to be more than just a straight how-to text. True, we had to have all the hard-core information about horsemanship, training and becoming a better rider, but he wanted to add more layers and another dimension that would "tell the tale" in each chapter. Therefore, you'll see several sidebars that help flush out the chapters' subject matter. The "Here's How's" offer tips on becoming a more skilled horseman. "A Better Way" sidebars provide workable solutions to common horse-handling problems that we all encounter.

The sidebars titled "True Story" are personal anecdotes from Craig's life and his experiences as a clinician, and they really hit home. Sometimes you can learn more from one good story than you can from a mountain of instructional text.

This book was fun for me to write and I learned a lot along the way. I hope you'll find the same. I think you will.

—*Kathy Swan*

# FOREWORD

My brother Craig has always been courageous. In grade school and high school, he was a fearless defensive back who never backed off from aggressive tackling, bigger running backs. When he was older, he rode bulls on the Professional Rodeo Cowboys Association circuit for 10 years. When he got hurt, sometimes severely, he always came back as soon as he healed. But the courage he showed in another way is the reason I most admire him. Let me explain.

Our Dad is an orthopedic surgeon, and we've lived in Houston most all our lives. However, our family was fortunate to have a ranch where we spent many weekends. The ranch had a lot of horses and among them was an extremely old horse named Mac. Because of his age and slow movement, Mac was perfect for small children. While my brother Doug and I enjoyed riding Mac, Craig loved riding Mac. Craig was only 5 years old but his fascination with horses and the western way showed through quite clearly. Craig literally couldn't get enough of riding, caring for and feeding that old horse.

In high school his love of the outdoors, horses and the western life continued to blossom. Craig often participated in local rodeos and worked on the ranch in the summer. What made this unusual is that many members of our family are doctors or lawyers. Craig's grandfather, grandmother, Dad, uncle, brother and cousin were one or the other. As you might guess, to diverge from that path isn't easy, but Craig did just that. I admire my brother because he had the courage to follow his true star and his real passion. Shakespeare wrote in Hamlet, "To thine own self be true." No one that I know exemplifies that more than Craig and everyone in the family is proud of him and happy for the joy he's found following his destiny.

—*Bruce Cameron, Jr.*

# INTRODUCTION

Legendary horseman Tom Dorrance once said: "Work on your horse by working on yourself." I've thought a lot about that. In reality, horses already know what to do. They know to walk, trot, canter, stop, back-up, turn right and turn left. You never have to teach a horse to do those things. What you've got to do is teach your horse where, when and how to do them, maybe even want to do them or even like to do them. You need a willing attitude on your horse's part.

The bottom line on what true horsemanship is: Communication. If I had to give one word to describe horsemanship. it would be that. How well can you get your horse to understand what it is you want him to do? How well can you get your horse to understand what it is you don't want him to do? That's horsemanship.

This book is all about better communication with the horse. Communication is two minds open and two minds listening. In the world of horsemanship, however, we've got to speak horse to the horse for that communication to take place. He's not going to learn to speak our language, so we're going to have to learn to speak his.

My goal has been to express this language to you in a way that makes it easy for you to understand and easy for you to help your horse understand. I don't want to make it any more complicated than it already is, but I don't want to promise you that it won't be a lot of work either. It is.

This book covers a lot of territory, from equine psychology to physiology, equipment to ground work, hobble-breaking to longe-line techniques, the first ride to advanced maneuvers and from equitation to trailer loading. My hope is that, along the way, you learn to become the best horseman or woman you can be and your horse learns to become the best man-horse he can be. I want you to be able to ride smart, so you can ride again tomorrow.

*Craig Cameron*

# CONTENTS

*"The horse is perfect for what he is and that is a horse."*

# 1
# NATURE OF THE HORSE

When it comes to horses and horsemanship, understanding the nature of the horse is one of the most important things you must learn. It's something you'll have to study and to get good at, because no one comes into the world understanding it. Your horse didn't come into the world understanding what you want of him, either; he's going to have to learn.

Learning takes time. Basically, it's a response to a demand for growth, to experience something new. Much of the time, as you interact with your horse, you'll ask him to deal with lots of things he's never done before. Just realize that it's not only a learning process for the horse, but for you as well. It boils down to learning how to speak horse to the horse. You have to get good enough at it so you can teach him.

## Predator/Prey

The nature of the horse is to be a prey animal — to be the hunted, not the hunter. Think of the horse as a pure survivor. He's an animal other animals eat; therefore, by nature, he's afraid. This instinct has kept him alive for 50 million years. Only the strong and wary survived to generate the horses we have now. You'll never take the instinct to survive out of the horse; don't even try. It's too important to him and ingrained too deeply. Let him figure out that he doesn't need to use it.

The nature of man is exactly opposite that of the horse. We're a predatory species. We're not usually the hunted; we're the hunters. Therefore, we think differently.

*Understanding the nature of the horse is all-important to becoming a good horseman.*

*As prey animals, horses are naturally afraid of predators, and humans are considered a predatory species. By developing a language you both can understand, first on the ground and then in the saddle, you take the fear out of the horse and turn that prey animal into your partner.*

You have to put yourself in your horse's place to really understand where he's coming from and why he's afraid. To a horse, anything can be a predator — rustling leaves or scary objects. He's always on guard; otherwise, he thinks he might be killed by the stalking predator.

Think of yourself swimming in shark-infested waters. That's the way the horse feels. He's afraid for one thing. He's afraid for his life. He's afraid he's going to get killed.

To help him survive, Mother Nature gave him four strong legs, big lungs, the gift of speed, and told him that anytime he even thinks there's a problem, run. That flight instinct might be buried deep in a domesticated, well-trained horse, but make no mistake, it's always there.

If, when working with your horse before he's ready or prepared, you take away his strongest instinct, that of flight, by tying him or hobbling him and he becomes afraid and can't run, or if you push too hard or fast or present things to him in a way he can't understand, he'll fight. He'll bite, kick, buck, paw, freeze up or do whatever

it takes to survive. He won't think; he'll react through instinct. If you fight with a horse, you're going to get a fight. Very quickly, you'll have nothing, and you'll be going backward in a hurry.

One of the most important things you should do to your horse every day, whether it's his first ride, 10th ride, 100th ride or 1,000th ride is to take the fear out of the horse, and, to a large extent, that's what this book is about. You'll find lots of advice and training techniques that'll help you work with your horse, not against him. You'll learn to take the fear out of your horse with careful, step-by-step riding foundation basics that build confidence and trust. By developing a language you both can understand, you'll be better able to communicate with your horse on his level. Your horse will look upon you as his leader and friend, not his enemy, a predator or someone he has to fear.

Man has never bred the instinct to survive — in other words, to be afraid — out of the horse. He'll naturally be afraid until you give him a reason not to be, and you do that by the way you handle him. Your horse might need to use his instincts to realize he doesn't need to use them. In other words, he might need to get scared to realize he doesn't need to be scared. For example, the first time a horse encounters a noisy motor vehicle, he might spook and try to flee. But as soon as he realizes that it won't hurt him, especially if his handler is calm and reassuring, he'll put it on his list of non-predatory objects.

The best time to start taking the fear out of a horse is at the beginning of his life. If you could be a part of your horse's life from the day he's born (a process called imprinting), he'd learn to trust that you're something he doesn't have to fear. Imprinting methods (sensitizing and desensitizing techniques) have proven very successful in socializing horses to humans. Renowned veterinarian Dr. Robert M. Miller is the all-time expert on this process and I highly

recommend reading his book, *Imprint Training of the Newborn Foal*, published by *Western Horseman.*

But if you weren't present at your horse's birth (and that's usually the case), then you need to learn to be a part of your horse's life and work with your horse in ways that won't scare him.

In time, a horse can learn to trust humans, but that trust can be easily destroyed. Fortunately, however, horses are extremely forgiving animals. If someone is rough on a horse, rides him poorly, disciplines him the wrong way, whips, scares him, and he still allows that person to catch and ride him, that's a forgiving animal. You don't want to betray that trust too many times. But horses are all such individuals. Some will keep coming back and continue to trust; others will never get over one bad

## HERE'S HOW

### Relax a Horse

This is one of my favorite ways to relax an overly anxious horse — one that shows a little fear of being handled. You should be able to touch your horse all over his body without him being afraid. This desensitizing exercise helps take the fear out of the horse.

Rub a long, soft, cotton rope all over the horse's body in a quiet, deliberate and rhythmic way. Run it up and down his legs and around his flanks, heart-girth, and hindquarters. If he's saddled, pop the stirrup leathers, pick up the back cinch, rock the saddle horn. Make sure the horse is comfortable with being handled all the way through his body. If the process spooks him, stop, wait and then start again. This "sacking out" helps him relax physically, mentally and emotionally.

*To desensitize and take the fear out of a horse, rub a soft cotton rope all over his body.*

incident. They just have a much stronger sense of self-preservation.

Never take it for granted that this prey animal allows a predator to ride on his back. That's an amazing fact. You sit up there for one reason only — through his good grace.

You're asking something of your horse. Your horse isn't asking anything of you, except a good deal. So try to think like a horse. Try to work with him as another horse would. When you do, the two of you will get along better.

## Herd Behavior

Like most prey animals, horses are herd animals. They travel in small bands for safety and companionship. There's safety in numbers when predators lurk. But every bit as important is the fact that horses are very social creatures, interacting with one another in a very strict and ordered society.

No matter how large or small the herd, horses develop a pecking order — a hierarchy or caste system in which the entire herd operates. They work through leadership. They learn their places in the pecking order and stay there until something changes. When one horse gets crippled, sick, weak or leaves the herd, then each horse moves up in the pecking order. There's always a dominant leader, a second-in-command horse, a third, a fourth and so on down the line.

Submissive horses are very content to be low on the totem pole. It doesn't bother them. It's just not very important to them, where it's more important or more instinctual for a dominant horse to be in charge.

Horses learn from one another and they're incredible disciplinarians. When two horses clash over food or breeding rights, they might fight; and while the squabble can be vicious at times, it's typically over with quickly. Usually, one horse yields. The next time it comes time to feed or breed, all the victor needs to do is pin his ears or turn his rump and the defeated horse will read the signs and give way.

*Horses are social animals and the herd instinct is one of the most ingrained in the equine.*

In developing a relationship with your horse, it would behoove you to mimic herd behavior in your own little herd of two. You can do so not by trying to work through pain or fear, but through understanding. Sometimes to achieve understanding, like the aggressive horse above, you'll have to use discipline or firmness, but the lessons should have positive effects.

Your discipline shouldn't be the enemy of your horse's enthusiasm. Don't discipline in a way that creates fear. For example, whipping a confused horse never accomplished anything, except to justify your horse's fear. He didn't understand what you wanted in the first place, and now all he knows is that he's afraid of you. He's convinced now that you're the predator. Your aggressive actions proved that to him.

One thing you should realize is that horses expect discipline. That's the way their society works. Offending horses get swift kicks or bites from their superiors. When the skirmish is over, law and order in the herd are restored. That's not to say that you should kick or in any way get rough with your horse, but realize that you might have to use firmness at the appropriate time.

Discipline in a way that creates respect. A sharp tug on the lead rope and a demand for the horse's attention are more effective than severe punishment. Let the horse tell you how much or how little discipline he needs. Correction is good, but encouragement is better.

## Leader of the Pack

Horses are easier to teach than people, because they have no ego to deal with. The horse doesn't care if you're the dominant one. He expects there to be a Number One. That's natural for him. You won't bruise his ego or embarrass him. He might test you. If he finds he can walk over you, run you off, get you to yield, then he'll do it. But if you assert yourself as the dominant one, he'll think, "Yep, you're the leader; that suits me fine." He'll know and accept his place in the pecking order. You didn't have to scare him to create that respect. You just had to work with him like another horse would, within the herd dynamics, in this case, within the herd of two.

You can't change a horse's nature. He might be naturally dominant or naturally submissive. You have to work with a horse

### True Story: The Instinct to Survive

*One night at our Double Horn Ranch in Bluffdale, Texas, my wife, Dalene, woke me and said, "Something outside is screaming." Being the middle of the night and Dalene not being an alarmist, this sent a shiver through me. It was spring and we had several mares ready to foal. I got up, put on my boots, jacket and hat and headed into the cold night armed with a gun and my flashlight.*

*I heard the scream and froze in my tracks. I ran as fast as I could to the mare corral. All the horses on the ranch seemed unraveled and were running about in a frantic way I'd never seen before. Again the scream pierced the cold night air. The closer I got, the more the high-pitched noise seemed like a frightened little voice with a "help me" sound threaded through it.*

*Entering the mare trap, I scanned the area with my flashlight and immediately found an embryo sack. I heard the little scream again and turned my light toward it. I saw a mare standing over her newborn foal whose hind legs were caught in the cable fencing that held the youngster captive. I quickly retrieved the tiny, vocal survivor, and to my surprise he was sound and strong. With mare in tow, I walked them to a warm stall. Luckily everything turned out fine. The little guy's big heart and strong vocal chords brought him through.*

*Today, I'm riding that horse and he's a dandy. His name is "Twister," and I have to admit that he gets a little preferential treatment at the ranch. He's a character. (Editor's note: Twister is featured in many of the book's photographs.)*

*I don't think I'll ever forget that scream in the night. It was a scream of survival, a scream of instinct. I truly believe that every horse on the ranch knew what it was, and the herd instinct was to try to help.*

*The instinct to survive is all-powerful in the horse. Be aware of what it is, why it is and don't try to take it away from him. Just let him figure out that he doesn't need to use it around you.*

*Your horse might test your leadership skills to find out who's the leader of the pack.*

*As soon as you make it clear you're No. 1 in the herd of two, the horse changes his attitude and for the better. He'll give you his full attention and respect.*

the way he is. Obviously, the way you'd deal with a dominant personality is different than what you'd do with a submissive one. The dominant horse might require more firmness from you just to get his attention and respect.

Many people have problems with "herd-bound" horses. You'll never meet a horse that isn't herd-bound in some way. That's natural for the species. If your horse doesn't have another horse to bond to, he might bond to you.

It's important when you work with your horse that you give him a reason to find solace and comfort with you like he would with other horses. If you don't spend enough time with your horse, if he spends too much time with the herd or his buddies, naturally the bond with them will be stronger.

You change that by becoming the leader when you're with your horse. You should recognize when your horse is in charge, when he takes over by ignoring you, by walking over you, by turning his rump to you, not giving you his attention. You can't train a horse unless you have his attention. You'll have to earn his attention, his respect, his confidence, his trust. These are things you can't make happen. You do it spending time with the horse and working with him correctly.

## Three Levels — Physical, Emotional, Mental

Some horses are physically, emotionally and mentally very sensitive and you can't change that. Always remember that you're dealing with a horse on all three levels. Most of us deal with horses physically — we handle them, we ride them; but we don't do a very good job dealing with them mentally and emotionally.

By mentally, I mean the mind, which controls the body, the legs and the feet. Your horse's legs and feet are what he uses to flee and fight with. If you control his mind, you've probably got control of his body, as well as his legs and feet. If you can't control his legs and feet, it's a pretty good indication that you don't have control of his mind either. A horse that bucks or runs off is a good example of a horse whose mind isn't under the control of his rider.

You're also dealing with your horse's emotions. He can get bothered, bored, scared, unsure, happy, troubled — all these things, and they all affect your relationship with your horse. For instance, within the herd, when one horse spooks, they all usually spook. So if you jump at something, your horse might very well jump too. If you're not afraid, then your horse will take his cue from you. Your horse will sense if you're sure or unsure. Ultimately, you want your horse to face his fears, not run away from them.

## The Need to Breed

The desire to propagate is great in all species, and you can't ignore that fact when it comes to horses. Often, when hormones take over and horses feel the need to breed, their personalities change and that can make them less reliable as riding partners. They can be different one day to the next. It's another one of those facts about equine nature that won't change, so you'll have to learn to deal with it.

The breeding instinct in a stallion is very strong. Never underestimate his powerful urges and dominant tendencies. The sweet horse you own and love can turn into a totally different animal when nature calls. Never turn your back on any stallion. One of the most important things to teach a stallion is when to breed and when not to breed.

PHOTO BY KATHY SWAN

*There's a social hierarchy in any herd. Often the foal of the dominant mare assumes her status in the herd.*

**15**

When a mare cycles, generally every 21 days, her personality might change, just like the stallion's, from day to day. Some mares never seem bothered by hormonal changes, but enough are that it warrants your investigation and understanding.

As all-around riding mounts, geldings make the best choice because they're consistent day in and day out. That's one reason why many ranches prefer them. You'll find that even in a mixed herd of geldings and mares, squabbling will take place. The eons-old herd social structure takes over and there usually will be one dominant gelding and one dominant mare. Although geldings are usually more dependable, some do act like stallions their whole lives.

Remember, though, when it comes to performance, you also get a little more "life" or energy with stallions and mares. Witness the high number of stallions and mares that populate the futurity finals of high-caliber performance events such as cutting, reining and working cow horse. Also, note that the vast majority of amateur and non-professional riders are mounted on geldings.

A related note on breeding: When you breed a mare to a stallion, you should look for the best traits of each - mentally as well as physically. Although the foal gets 50 percent from each parent, he lives the first 6 months of his life with his dam. He'll pick up a lot of the mare's personality characteristics. If the mare is bossy or has a poor disposition toward people or other horses, many times the foal will pick up on that. He'll imitate the mare, even learn to assume her place in the pecking order. You can see this at the watering hole. The dominant mare always drinks first and her foal will bat his ears at any intruders until she's done drinking. The foal thinks that's the natural way of things. Him first, other horses second. Try to select broodmares who have good dispositions, good minds, who relate to people and other horses in a good way.

## Do Horses Love?

I think horses have their own form of love or affection. Watch a mare with her foal and listen to her softly nicker to him. I think the worst to fall in love with each other are the geldings. I've seen many a gelding fall in love with his stablemate.

But horses can have affection for humans, too. For example, at the huge horse expos that attract thousands of people, I can just walk up to my horses' stalls and maybe it's the sound of my spurs or if I give a little whistle, my horses start nickering. They look for me to reach their stalls.

If you ride a horse right, if you train him right, if you have a relationship with your horse, he'll meet you at the gate. I've had horses chase me down the road, upset because they weren't in the trailer going with me.

Once I went to a barrel racing clinic at Martha Josey's and saw a teenage girl riding a white horse everywhere — between the trailers, all over the place. I thought that maybe she should give the horse a break. But then I noticed her horse was having as much fun as she was. Later on, I watched her run the barrels on the horse and she was able to do it sitting backward. She did it backward better than most of the other girls did it riding frontward. I realized that she had truly developed a relationship with her horse.

So, I think your horse can learn to love you, especially if you spend enough time with him. You can become an important member of the horse's herd. You can become his herd leader.

## Intelligence

The horse has an incredible mind and an equally extraordinary memory. However, you can never teach horses mathematics because they're not geared that way mentally. They're not on the same intelligence scale as human beings. Intelligence is relative in all species, and horses have their own form of intelligence. It's more instinctual. Something you don't have to think about is instinctive, and horses' instincts have been honed for millions of years. I don't know how good a horse's ability to reason is, but

I've always said the horse is perfect for what he is and that's a horse.

Horses learn the tasks we want them to learn through repetition. You might have to do something over and over 100 times before your horse understands it. You just have to be patient. Patience is waiting without worry. Remember that the horse didn't come into this world knowing what you want. He has to figure it out through repetition.

Frankly, horses probably wonder why it is we want them to do certain things. They really don't comprehend the logic of the things we ask of them. It's our job to make it clear.

A lot of what you teach your horse is through feel — a touch with your hands, bits, reins, legs and spurs. In training, unless there's a reason, meaning or purpose, don't pick up on the lead rope or reins, or press on your horse with your hands, reins, legs, bits or spurs. In time, through repetition and consistency, your horse will begin to see the reason, meaning and purpose of what you're doing to him. When you can communicate at the highest level, though, you won't need the bits, spurs or reins. I think horses are totally capable of learning to that degree.

Most of the time, we barely scratch the surface of what we can ask horses to do. We don't ask them to do enough of the things they're capable of; therefore we don't see the extent of their type of intelligence. But look at the unbelievable things some circus and movie trainers do with their horses — work at liberty, remember complicated routines, canter backward. They're good enough horsemen to teach it, and they have the patience to achieve it.

But as I said earlier, great training can occur only when you take the fear out of the horse. He can't learn if he's afraid. You have to overcome his instinct of fear first. Then his mind will open, and you'll be amazed at what he can learn.

Just remember that learning is a two-way street. It's two minds opening, two minds listening and two minds communicating. When you learn to talk horse to every horse you handle, you're on your way to becoming a horseman.

*Cutting horses are bred to be "cow-smart," which means they have the innate ability to handle cattle. The trainer's job is to bring out that talent in the horse. But once the trainer or rider lays his rein hand down, he expects the horse to be smart enough to outthink the cow without his help. That's one form of equine intelligence at work.*

*Reining horses are bred to not outthink the rider. A top reiner is "willingly guided or controlled...and dictated to completely." (National Reining Horse Association Handbook) In this sport, riders look for horses that are talented enough to learn the complicated maneuvers, yet possess the type of intelligence and disposition that allows them to wait for the rider's commands.*

**17**

# A BETTER WAY

## The Blue Tarp Monster

For some reason, horses are frightened of plastic, especially the blue plastic tarps we use to cover things. Here's what I do to overcome a horse's fear of that scary object. This exercise helps horses get over their fears of many things.

*1. Fold the plastic tarp into a manageable size, such as a small square or long rectangle, and rub it all over the horse.*

*2. Unfold the tarp and shake it at and around the horse.*

*3. Rub the tarp all over his body again. If it scares him, take it away and start over.*

*4. Let him wear it on his body like a blanket for awhile until he's comfortable with it.*

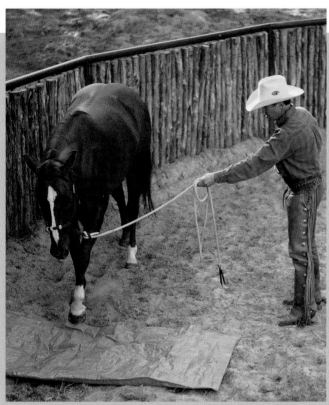

5. Fold the tarp into a long rectangle and lay it lengthwise along the side of a round pen. Ask the horse to longe around in circles. He'll probably stop in front of the tarp or avoid it all together. Don't force him over the tarp; let him inspect it on his own.

6. When he's comfortable with it in the pen, open it up a little more at a time until the tarp is totally open. Let him check it out as often as he feels the need.

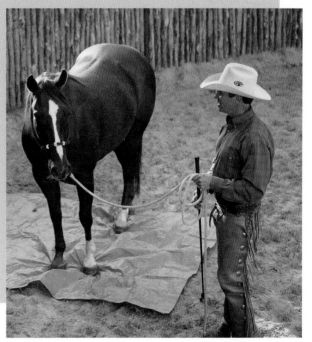

7. Longe him again, asking him to move over it. He might try to jump it. That's okay.

8. At some point, when the horse lands on the tarp, ask him to stop and stand on it. Do so by removing the pressure: Step back and quiet your movement and voice.

*"When a horse kicks, bites or bucks you off, he'll never say he's sorry."*

# 2
# READING THE HORSE

A horse's body is very expressive; it telegraphs every emotion and thought a horse has. By being able to decipher these "expressions," and knowing what they are in the first place, you can tell what's on your horse's mind. You'll know what he's thinking, feeling and even what he's going to do next. Horses never do something without first preparing to do it, and sometimes that preparation can be lightning fast. But if you know what the "signs" mean, you can prepare for your horse's actions.

## Body Language

How a horse holds his body says a lot about what's going through his mind at the time.

When he stands statuesque, stiff, with his head up, he's on guard; he's alert to something in his environment. His natural instincts tell him to pay attention to potential danger. If he perceives trouble, his feet will start moving and he'll be out of there. His first reaction is to run; but if he can't leave, he could charge, bite, paw or kick to defend himself.

When he lowers his head in a relaxed or natural way, he's turned loose physically, mentally and emotionally. He's comfortable with his surroundings and sees no danger. Usually at the same time he drops his head he'll wiggle his ears and lick his lips — all signs of relaxation. A confident horse usually carries his head in a relaxed position. Look at horses in the pasture. Ninety percent of them have their heads down to graze. This is a natural position for them and means they're relaxed and happy

*Horses in a herd situation are constantly talking to one another with their body language and facial expressions.*

with their world. They'll raise their heads for something alarming.

When a horse turns his hindquarters toward another horse or a human, it's a threatening gesture. He's saying he's displeased and might kick if the human or that other horse doesn't back away. He might even lift his leg in a mock kick. He's just one step away from the real thing when he does that. Be careful.

With ears pricked forward, the horses in the front row see something interesting in the distance. Horses' body language is very expressive. You can often tell what's on a horse's mind by the way that the horse stands.

When he trots or canters, a horse sometimes holds his tail out from his body as part of his balancing mechanism.

## Ears

Horses use their ears not only to listen, but also to talk. They're like a radio antenna, really telegraphing what's going on with the horse, and the different positions a horse can put them in speak volumes about what the horse is thinking.

When you see a horse grazing in the pasture raise his head and gaze in the distance, look where he's gazing. His ears will be pointed straight forward at whatever has his attention. It might be another horse or coyotes or something, but he's on the alert, he's inquisitive, he hears something he thinks he needs to investigate. In the wild or in a pasture situation, an alert horse decides whether to run from danger.

When a horse pins his ears, he's angry, disgruntled or upset. Pay attention because he might prepare to charge, kick, bite, paw or do any other offensive or defensive move. Pinned ears is a sign of displeasure and a threat. The horse is signaling his intention to do something about what's bothering him.

If you're trail riding with friends and the horse in front of you pins his ears, watch out. He doesn't want you that close to him, and he might kick your horse. If you're riding a horse that pins his ears, be aware that he might kick the horse behind or beside him. Move your horse's hindquarters away and warn the rider behind you. Don't just be a passenger on your horse, be a proactive rider.

Horses can point their ears in two different directions at the same time. One ear might be pointed forward, paying attention to what's ahead, and the other ear might be pointed backward, monitoring the rider or what's behind.

## Tail

A horse's tailbone is actually an extension of his spine, but a horse can express himself through his tail. You can tell what a horse is feeling by watching the position of his tail. A relaxed horse lays his tail against his body in a natural manner when standing still or walking. When being ridden at the trot or canter, he sometimes holds it slightly

# HERE'S HOW

### Tail Lift

A horse should be gentle from the first whisker of his nose to the last hair in his tail. Be sure that you can touch your horse all over his body, including his tail. You might have to take his temperature some day and being able to handle his tail makes the whole process easier.

The tension in your horse's tail also can tell you something about your horse's level of resistance. With your hand, reach underneath your horse's tailbone and try to lift the tail. Most horses resist this action to different degrees and clamp their tails — the stronger-willed or nervous horses more so than the complacent and agreeable creatures.

Keep holding the tail until the horse softens it and relaxes and allows you to lift it up and away from his body. When he does, that means he's "turned loose" and accepts what you're doing and that you're in charge. Then you can lower it.

You can begin this process with imprinting the day a foal is born.

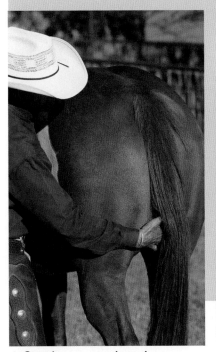

1. Start low on your horse's hindquarters, at the end of the horse's tailbone.

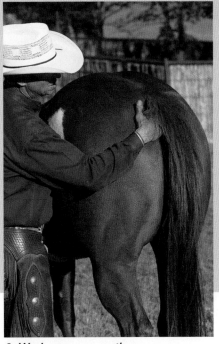

2. Work your way up the tailbone slowly. Most horses clamp their tails in resistance.

3. Wait for your horse to relax his tailbone and try to lift his tail in the air.

out from his body as a balancing mechanism. A scared horse tucks or clamps his tail against his body. And an excited and generally happy horse lifts his tail high like a flag.

An unhappy horse swishes his tail. On the trail, a horse might swish his tail at the horse behind him as a warning that that horse is too close. In the show ring, horses that swish their tails are probably unhappy with their jobs or hurting. Some exhibitors deaden their horses' tails with alcohol or some sort of numbing blocks so the tail can't move or move as well. I think that's cruel. The tail is important to the horse. Besides helping him balance (since it's a part of his spine), he uses it to communicate to other horses and to swat flies.

## Pay the Consequences

The consequences of not paying attention to a horse's body language, ears and tail can be painful. If you've never been kicked, bitten, run over or bucked off by a horse, you probably haven't handled many horses. Always look at it as a learning experience.

One of the interesting things about a horse is that when he kicks, bites or bucks you off, he'll never say he's sorry. He has no apologies and no regrets. That's the nature of the horse. You can't change it. The horse probably said:

"Didn't you see me? I've been trying to tell you something and you didn't listen." Horses are honest; they don't lie, but they'll surprise you. It's your job to be aware of what they are trying to tell you.

Walk into a pasture full of mares and foals and watch the mares pin their ears at you to stay away. You'd better beware. If you walk into your horse's stall and he turns his butt to you, stop. He's showing his disrespect for you and telling you to leave him alone. If you keep coming, he might kick.

Don't ignore your horse's body expressions. Your horse is trying to communicate with you. Be horseman enough to listen, be aware and give your horse the reason to change.

PHOTO BY KATHY SWAN

*Horses can point their ears in two directions at the same time, keeping abreast of what's going on around them.*

## True Story: Fix it Sooner Rather Than Later

*At one of my clinics, a participant had a horse that turned away from her in the round pen, pinned back both ears and ran backward at the handler.*

*I thought this was a problem that could be corrected with some help. And the horse owner was at the right place to get some help. It took a little discipline to correct the horse. It didn't take much, but I had to be firm with that horse to get her to yield her head laterally and give in the hindquarters. With a little time and patience, I did fix the horse's dangerous problem.*

*Another participant, who didn't even own the horse, thought I was being too hard on the horse. She felt sorry for a horse who was trying to hurt or kill someone. I couldn't understand that. I*
asked her if she'd ever seen anyone who'd been kicked in the head or chest by a horse? What about someone crippled or, worse, turned into a vegetable or even killed by a horse, instantly? So the owner needed to fix the problem or sell the horse, one of the two, because if she didn't, her horse would seriously hurt her someday.

*The moral of this story is that if your horse is giving you a dangerous problem, you either handle it yourself immediately, ask a pro to help you or get rid of the horse. Don't feel sorry for the horse because the horse will never feel sorry for you. Either you help the horse make the change or you get rid of him. There are too many good horses out there to put up with an outlaw. If the horse can't or won't be fixed, then he might very well hurt someone someday and end up at the slaughterhouse anyway. It's like having a bad kid. Either you discipline him yourself or the police will.*

# A BETTER WAY

## Butt to You

A horse that pins his ears when you enter his stall, turns his rump to you and, in general, has a poor attitude toward you is definitely showing his disrespect. He thinks he's higher on the pecking order than you. You need to take control of this situation, because at some point the horse might also kick.

Never walk up to a horse that has his rump toward you. Do something to make him face you. Smooch at the horse to get his attention and, if he doesn't respond, flick your lead rope at his hindquarters, kick some bedding at him, do something to get him to turn and face you, so it's safe to put on his halter. Repeat until he turns to face you. Then, and only then, approach the horse.

2. Flick the end of your lead rope, smooch, cluck, kick dirt or do something to make the horse face you.

1. Never approach a horse when his hindquarters are turned toward you. This horse is trying to escape being caught and haltered.

3. The safest time to handle a horse is when he faces you. This horse now shows respect for and acceptance of the handler.

# 3
# MECHANICS OF THE HORSE

The mechanics of the horse revolve around how the horse is built and how his body works, just as the nature of the horse pertains to the horse's psyche and how the horse's mind works. Equine mechanics deal with the way in which the horse moves across the earth. A horse drives from behind, turns on his center and pulls with his front. The better you understand how a horse moves, the better you'll be able to understand how to control his feet.

Riding is communicating with the horse's mind to control the horse's feet. When you want a horse to go to the right, you must have his feet go to the right. When you want a horse to back, you have to get his feet to move backward. When you want a horse to load into a trailer, you must first get his feet into the trailer.

When you understand where your horse's feet are at all times, you better understand your horse and, therefore, become a better horseman.

## Breeding and Conformation

When looking at a prospect for the kind of riding you want to do, ask yourself if the horse is bred to perform the tasks he needs to do and if he's physically capable of doing them. For example, if you want to ride in endurance races, get a horse that's bred for long-distance work, such as the Arabian. If you're looking for a smooth-riding trail horse, check into the gaited breeds, such as Missouri Fox Trotters or Paso Finos. If

*A horse with good conformation usually moves beautifully.*

**27**

PHOTO BY KATHY SWAN

*Because of their conformation and endurance capabilities, Arabians are the breed of choice for long-distance riding.*

*Race-bred Quarter Horses, with their swift bursts of speed and ability to stop and turn quickly, make outstanding barrel-racing mounts.*

*This reining horse can stop hard and slide on his rear end while still pedaling with his front legs because he has heavily muscled hindquarters and a light front end. Also, note his clean throatlatch, which allows him to flex at the poll.*

*Equine athletes need to be structurally sound to perform. This cutting-horse stallion exhibits many traits of a well-conformed horse.*

competing in speed events is your game, a good bet would be a race-bred Quarter Horse. And if you want to work cattle, it makes sense to consider a Quarter Horse with cutting-horse bloodlines.

Through selective breeding, horsemen have carefully and purposefully bred certain physical and mental characteristics into the gene pools of today's modern equine breeds, giving riders the best chance of success in whatever sport they choose.

Conformation becomes really important in any type of performance. The better a horse is put together, the easier it is for him to do what's required. Take reining as an example. It's hard for a horse that's heavy on the front end, thick-necked or slight in the hindquarters to perform the spectacular sliding stops reining horses are known for. Those stops require horses that are refined and balanced in their necks, light in their front ends (so they can lift them in the classic reiner's pedaling motion) and heavily muscled in the hindquarters to hold the ground and slide — over and over again.

In general, however, a good horse is a good horse, and good conformation is good conformation.

Here are some conformational points common to all good horses:

· A pretty, refined head with big soft eyes, large nostrils and an alert look. A soft, "gentle" eye can say a lot about a horse's character.

· A refined neck in proportion to the horse's body, one that comes out of the shoulders level, neither too high nor too low. A clean throatlatch makes it easy for the horse to break at the poll and therefore give to the bit.

· A balanced body in the shape of a trapezoid, meaning the back is short, the underline long; slanting shoulder and hip angles should match. A well-balanced body is an athletic one.

· Good height to the withers, to hold a saddle in place.

· A big heart girth for heart and lung capacity.

· Strong loins and hindquarters for maximum power and stability.

· Straight legs, with good bone, a short cannon bone.

· Good oval-shaped hooves, large enough to support the horse's weight.

**Walk – four beats.** *Front-foot sequence. To show the four-beat walk effectively in a photographic sequence, the foot that's lifted is the one about to be put down on the ground.*

*First beat — counting with the front feet, the sequence begins with the right front.*

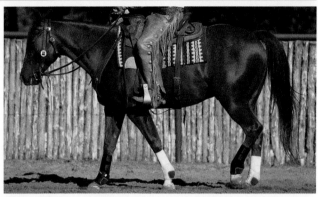

*Second beat — left hind.*

*Third beat — left front.*

*Fourth beat — right hind.*

# The Gaits

Understanding the sequence in which a horse picks up his feet helps you get more in rhythm with him. For example, if he were to pick up his right front foot and you knew which foot he was going to pick up next, that would help you prepare to stop, turn or back him.

The vast majority of horses move in three gaits: a four-beat walk, a two-beat trot and a three-beat canter. In the case of many gaited breeds, the trot is replaced by a four-beat lateral gait (see below).

## Walk

The walk is a four-beat gait and I think it's one of the most interesting gaits of all. A large part of my training program is done at a walk and a trot. In a walk, the horse is relaxed. He moves slowly, and it's easier to teach him then than when he's moving faster.

*Sequence:* If you count each of the four beats starting with the front feet, the pattern is: right front foot, left hind foot, left front foot, right hind foot. But if you start counting with the hind feet, the pattern would be: right hind, right front, left hind, left front.

## Trot and Back-Up

The trot is a two-beat diagonal gait in which the horse's diagonal pairs of legs move together.

*Sequence:* The left hind and right front foot move together; the right hind and left front foot move in unison.

The back-up also is a diagonal gait. It has the same movement sequence as the trot, but in reverse. When a horse picks up his right front foot to move backward, he also picks up the left hind foot. When he picks up the left front foot, he picks up the right hind foot at the same time.

**Hind-foot sequence.**

*First beat — counting with the hind feet, the sequence begins with the right hind.*

*Second beat — right front.*

*Third beat — left hind.*

*Fourth beat — left front.*

Often, horses don't perform the back-up correctly under saddle. Instead of moving in a two-beat gait, as described, they drag their feet backward one at a time. Rider error is usually the problem. The rider literally tries to pull the horse backward by hauling on the bit, instead of asking the horse to back with proper cues and releasing the rein pressure as the horse moves his feet.

## Canter or Lope

The canter (or lope) is a three-beat gait, with a diagonal phase (see below) and a leading leg. Horses are either in a right or left lead, meaning the right or left front leg appears to be leading the other three. There's also an airborne or suspension phase to the canter.

*Left-lead sequence:* In the first beat, the horse pushes off with the right hind foot. In the second beat, the left hind leg and right front leg move together, striking the ground simultaneously. The left front leg is in mid-air, appearing to be leading the other three legs, hence the word "lead." The third beat is the left front or leading leg striking the ground. After it hits the ground, all four legs

# A BETTER WAY

### Pick Up the Pace

Here's a way to get your horse to increase his pace at a walk. However, you can do this transition work at all gaits.

1. At a walk, use the rhythm in your own body to speed up your horse's pace without pushing him into a trot.

2. See how fast you can walk your horse and how long he'll carry this rhythm.

3. Now slow your body way down and see how slow your horse can walk without stopping.

In this exercise, you work through a feel and teach your horse to follow that rhythm or feel.

**Trot – two beats.** *In showing the trot, we note the two diagonal feet solidly on the ground.*

*First beat — right front, left hind.*

*Second beat — left front, right hind.*

*First beat — right front, left hind.*

*Second beat — left front, right hind.*

leave the ground in the airborne phase until the right rear lands again to begin the sequence.

***Right-lead sequence:*** In the first beat, the horse pushes off with the left hind leg. The second beat is the right hind and left front legs moving together. The third beat is the right front foot striking the ground. After it hits the ground, then the horse is airborne until the left hind leg strikes the ground again.

A horse changes leads in the airborne phase and, therefore, that's the best time to ask him to change from one lead to another. That's why it's called "flying lead change." (More about this in Chapter 17.)

## Diagonals

With the trot being a diagonal gait, you often "post" to the horse's two-beat motion, meaning you rise and fall in the saddle with a particular set of diagonal legs. This makes

riding the trot more comfortable for you and your horse. Posting is a movement that puts you in rhythm with your horse, so you're not bouncing on his back.

When you post, you're either on the right or left diagonal. If you're riding for miles cross-country, you should change diagonals periodically. That makes it less tiring for your horse, who can then support your weight equally on both pairs of diagonal legs.

Have you ever heard the expression "Rise and fall with the leg to the wall?" Did you ever wonder what that means and why? In posting the trot in an arena situation, you should post the correct diagonal for the direction you're traveling. The "wall" leg is the outside front leg nearest the wall or rail. If you're traveling to the right, you should post or rise up when the outside or left front leg (nearest the wall) and corresponding diagonal right hind leg move forward and sit down when they strike the ground. When you sit that

*Back-Up – two beats. The back-up has the same footfall sequence as the trot, only in reverse. To show the back-up effectively, the two feet lifted are about to be put down on the ground.*

*First beat — left front, right hind.*

*Second beat — right front, left hind.*

*First beat — left front, right hind.*

*Second beat — right front, left hind.*

beat, the right leg (closest to the inside of the arena) and the left hind leg come forward.

The reverse is true for traveling to the left in an arena. You should post or rise up when the right front leg, which is the leg nearest the wall, and the left hind leg move forward, and sit down when they strike the ground.

Although a three-beat gait, the canter also has a diagonal phase. In the first beat of a left-lead canter, your horse pushes off with the right hind leg. The second beat is the left hind and right front moving together in a diagonal motion. If you're posting the trot, that is, rising and falling with the leg to the wall, in this case the right front leg, it's easier to cue your horse to take a left lead during the correct diagonal phase of the trot.

## Lateral Gaits

A diagonal trot produces a side-to-side, two-beat gait that is naturally bouncy, hence riders sometimes choose to post rather than be jarred at the trot.

In addition to diagonal gaits, there are lateral gaits, common to "gaited" horses. There are various versions, but the most common is the pace, in which the hoofs on each side of the horse strike the ground together. The sequence is right front and right hind in the first beat, then left front and left hind in the second beat. Standardbred racehorses are either trotters or pacers. The trotters

# HERE'S HOW

### Feel the Diagonal

It's easy to see what diagonal you're posting by watching the movement of your horse's shoulders and front legs. But train yourself to "feel" the diagonal by closing your eyes and feeling the horse move underneath you. This is best accomplished when circling, rather than trotting a straight line.

**Canter or Lope – three beats.** *A canter or lope is a three-beat gait with a moment of suspension. In this left-lead sequence, we note the legs as they strike the ground.*

*First beat — right hind leg pushes off.*

*Second beat — left hind leg and right front leg strike ground simultaneously as a diagonal pair. Note the left front or leading leg in mid-air.*

*Third beat — the left front or leading leg strikes the ground.*

*Suspension — all four legs are momentarily suspended in mid-air. Note the right hind leg is about to touch down and push off to repeat the sequence.*

*The suspension phase of the gallop is obvious in this shot of a reining horse.*

race in the diagonal gait and the pacers race in a lateral pace.

Gaited horses, such as Tennessee Walking Horses, Missouri Fox Trotters and the Paso breeds, ride smoothly because their "gait" isn't a two-beat diagonal trot. Instead, the vast majority of them perform a broken pace, best described as a four-beat lateral movement in which the legs on the same side move in near unison. In other words, the legs on each side of the horse move together, but slightly independently of one another. At any one time, three legs are always on the ground. This produces a shuffling action that's easy to sit. The four-beat, lateral sequence is: right hind, right front, left hind, left front.

The American Saddlebred is a five-gaited horse. Besides walk, trot and canter, these horses perform a "slow gait" (broken pace) and a faster version called the "rack."

## Watch a Horse Move

One of the best places to watch a horse move is in a round pen, where you can observe his gaits closely. Standing in the middle of the pen offers you the best vantage point. You also learn a lot about how he moves naturally without a rider's interference.

*Walk:* At the walk, see how far the horse reaches up underneath himself with his hind legs. That will tell how much propulsion or drive from behind the horse has naturally. With any type of performance you want a horse that drives deeply underneath itself for maximum power.

*Trot:* At the trot, observe the horse's knee action. Do the knees move up and down like pistons or barely break at the knee joint at all?

Most western performance riders refer to the latter as a "flat-kneed horse," one who keeps his legs close to the ground. They prefer this type of efficient motion for the sports they do — reining, cutting, barrel racing, western pleasure, etc. Most flat-kneed horses appear to have a level top line when they move, which also is a desirable characteristic in the show pen. It presents a pretty picture to the judge, one that says a horse is smooth and comfortable to ride.

However, in some horse show events, such as Arabian or Morgan park-horse classes, horses with high knee action are rewarded. The higher, the better. Neither one is right or wrong; it's just whatever you want to do with your horse. As I said before, choose the breed or type of horse that best suits your style of riding.

*Canter or lope:* When you ask a horse to canter or lope, see if he picks up the correct lead naturally. In other words, when traveling to the left, he should pick up the left lead and when traveling to the right, the right lead. Ask him to change directions and he should also change leads.

Ask him to stop (by stepping in close to his front end) and see if he stops on his hindquarters. Or does he stop hard on his front end? What you're looking for in an athlete or performance horse is one that stops naturally on his hindquarters.

## Be Aware

The more you are aware of your horse's movement, the more you'll be in rhythm with your horse. Awareness is the beginning of all learning. It's the ability to see, hear, sense and feel all the little things that are around you all the time. A horse is constantly aware. You need to be aware of what your horse is doing, so you can go with him or correct him.

The more you're aware of the mechanics of the horse, the better horseman you'll be.

### True Story: Old Jim

*I used to rope wild cattle for a living and my favorite horse for that job was a thick-made, squatty little horse named Jim. The other cowboys used to laugh at old Jim because of the way he was made. But they didn't laugh long when they saw the way he could hold and drag big, tough cattle. Heck, he was just made for that job. His conformation and low center of gravity made it easy for him to handle those cattle. To this day, if I have a tough cow to work, I still think about old Jim.*

*Find a horse that suits your needs and goals and remember, pretty is as pretty does.*

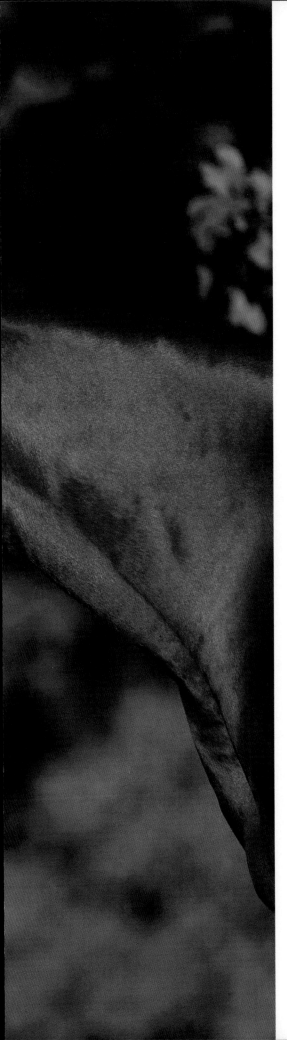

*"Great horsemen consistently ride good horses because their horses are a reflection of them."*

# 4

# THEORIES AND PHILOSOPHIES OF HORSEMANSHIP

The fundamentals of all good horsemanship are the same. It doesn't matter what seat or discipline or style of equitation you ride. You can take dressage principles and apply them to your western horse. A good horseman is a good horseman in any saddle, just as a good horse is a good horse, no matter the breed.

Great horsemen consistently ride good horses because their horses are a reflection of them. It's been said that the horse seeks the level of the rider. I think there's a lot of truth to that. One rider can get on a horse and get nothing out of the animal, while another rider can accomplish a lot because he presents things to the horse in a way the horse can understand. Any time you see a good horseman, try to learn from him, no matter the discipline, whether it's reining, western pleasure, dressage or jumping.

## Definition of Horsemanship

Horsemanship can be simply stated:

*Horse + man (or woman) = relationship.*

In every phase of horsemanship — on the ground or in the saddle — you have a relationship with your horse. Whether it's any good or not depends on you, not your horse. It's up to

*On the road to becoming a good horseman, you must first develop a good relationship with your horse, based on trust, respect and understanding.*

you to build a solid, working partnership. Your horse isn't going to do it for you.

I've always said that the horse is perfect for what he is and that's a horse. He doesn't have to do or change anything. In perfecting our relationship with him, we, as humans, must understand the animal's nature and mechanics and present ourselves to the horse in a way he can comprehend. Realize that horsemanship is all about working on yourself, not so much working on the horse. The horse is a rhythmical, balanced, patient, trusting and consistent animal. It's you who needs to develop feel, timing, rhythm, balance, patience, consistency and understanding.

The following theories and philosophies behind horsemanship are something to think about and let soak in over time. As you advance in your horsemanship knowledge and skills, their full and true meaning will become more meaningful to you.

## Feel

One of the first and most important things you must cultivate is feel. It's also one of the most difficult because it's a hard concept to describe and no one can give it to you. A good book to read about feel is a book titled *True Horsemanship Through Feel*, by Bill Dorrance and Leslie Desmond, published by Diamond Lu Productions.

Feel is more than just a physical touch; it's also an emotional response and a

*Developing a feel is an important aspect of good horsemanship. For example, as soon as your horse gives to the bit, release your pressure. That's how to develop feel. When your horse gives willingly to you, give back to him instantly.*

# A BETTER WAY

## Spend Time with Your Horse

The hard-to-catch horse is a common problem for many people. When someone tells me his horse is hard to catch, I ask him if the only time he catches his horse is to ride him. Horses are smart about this. It doesn't take one long to figure that out, and it doesn't take him long to figure out that he's a lot faster than his two-legged counterpart.

Give horses credit for thinking. They're definitely thinkers and full of common sense. Being able to figure out that he's faster than a human is really simple for any horse.

The trick to catching your horse is to spend more time with him. Don't make every time you're together a riding session. You can groom, bath, clip, graze him, any number of different things that don't involve riding.

For example, spend time with your horse out in the pasture. Don't catch him at all, simply pet or scratch him. Let him know that every time you show up it doesn't mean that he'll be caught.

*Have a little one-on-one with your horse without riding him. Visit him in his stall or pasture. Take time to scratch him or just be with him.*

mental approach to whatever situation you find yourself in with your horse.

Learning to do anything — dancing, playing a guitar, swinging a golf club — takes time and no one can really make you understand it or do it. They can teach you the fundamentals, but you'll have to create your own style and feel.

It's the same in horsemanship. You'll have to develop your own lightness and understanding of the horse, or feel. For example, when your horse is giving to the bit in response to one of your requests, the most important thing you can do is give back or release the pressure you placed on the horse. The release is the only thing in it for the horse. What you're trying to say to the horse is: "When you give, I'll give." That's a feel. "When you're soft, I'm soft." That's a feel. "When you yield, I yield." That's a feel. It's something you're going to have to work on over a period of time. Be

patient with yourself. Be patient with your horse. It's about give and take and truly a game of feel.

You can recognize that you're developing feel by your horse's responses. It'll take time for you to learn when to use more pressure and when to use less. In the beginning it might take a lot, but in the end it should take less. The result is a feel that's more of a suggestion and finally just a thought.

## Experience

Experience is the best teacher for feel. And if you want to experience horsemanship, you have to live it. You have to read about it, study it, make it your passion. You have to love it. Even if you don't have a horse, you can hang around a stable and clean stalls. Sit in the stands at horse events, watch and become a part of the horse industry. You can associate with people who're involved in it. Make it your lifestyle. Pretty soon you'll be able to grow. How can you be better if you're not willing to put in the time and work? It's your job to get the experience.

If you're lucky enough to have a horse, become a part of his life. Don't just catch him when you want to ride him. Go into his stall or corral, pet him, scratch behind his ears and hang out with your horse. Make it so he's happy to see you coming. You don't want your horse to run away; you want him to come to you. Be with your horse like another horse would. All the time you'll be learning from him. That's how you become a horse-man, and your horse becomes a man-horse. Your horse will get in tune with you.

Don't think of a horse as just a thing. He's not a tractor. He is a living, breathing entity, just like you. Learning horsemanship is like learning another language. You've got to become bilingual and speak horse to the horse.

## Timing

Timing is everything. Your timing has to be good in order to communicate with the horse on his level. Timing is discipline and timing is release. You have to know when to release pressure so the horse has an incentive to learn what you want. It's not the amount of pressure you place on the reins or spurs; it's the release the horse is interested in. It's the release that makes them responsive and light. Bits and spurs work on pressure and if you pull or push hard enough they work on pain. It's not the pressure or pain that gives the horse the incentive, it's the release. Horsemanship, like all things athletic, is a matter of feel, timing and balance.

Realize that time is not a concept horses understand. A horse never thinks in terms of time — of minutes or hours. That's a human thing. I've never seen a horse wear a watch. They live in the moment. Time to

the horse is time to eat, time to breed, time to move, time to sleep, length of day or night; that's time to a horse.

## Rhythm

Rhythm is a specific pattern of movement. Good horsemanship is getting in sync with your horse's movement. In any of the horse's gaits, there's a rhythm, and you need to move with it. They don't call it sitting, they call it riding.

It's like dancing. You and your horse are partners. Even if one person (you) is leading and one person (the horse) is following, ideally you're still moving together. As your horse's partner, it's your responsibility to be in rhythm with your horse's feet. It comes down to footwork.

## Balance

Balance is a state of equilibrium. You shouldn't hinder or impede your horse's movement with unbalanced riding, which would upset his equilibrium. Be in balance with your horse as you sit in the saddle — not too far forward, nor too far back. Don't lean from side to side. Move with your horse and not against him. A balanced rider helps, not hinders, a horse through all movements. You're riding a living entity; stay centered. The importance of balance in all maneuvers can never be overemphasized. It's a key ingredient in all great horsemanship.

Riding bareback will help you develop your balance. (See Chapter 8, "Bareback Riding.")

## Attitude

Develop a positive attitude about riding and horsemanship. It makes no sense to walk out to your horse's pen if you're looking for a fight. Consider yourself lucky and privileged if you get to ride only once a week or once a month. You're lucky to be around horses.

Your attitude has to be positive because your horse has the ability to pick up on your attitude. He has that awareness, the ability to sense whether you're feeling aggressive or mean or unsure. If you're having a bad day and having trouble adjusting your attitude, make sure you do something with your horse that's easy for you and your horse to do. Don't push the situation by tackling some difficult task.

Whatever you do, don't get angry at your horse; it will only get in your way. Don't get frustrated; frustration will only get in your way. You have to have more discipline and maturity than the horse. You can work your horse through inspiration or desperation. It's up to you. The greatest horsemen in the world get the most out of every horse because they have the right attitude.

Remember, horsemanship is a thinking and a working man's game. You've got to be able to work at it and outthink your horse. When a problem arises with a horse, stop and think it out.

## Look for the Try

What you look for in horsemanship is the try on the part of the horse. I'll accept anything but the quit from a person or a horse. I can't stand the word *can't*. Don't give me the can't; give me the try. Don't always expect 100 percent from your horse as long as he's trying. Be willing to accept only 75 percent of what you know he's capable of because you know he's trying.

Maybe he's just having a bad day. Horses are going to have good and bad days, just like you and me. Maybe your horse doesn't feel well today. Maybe he's hurting in places you're not aware of. If you accept your horse's 75 percent today, maybe he'll give you 110 percent tomorrow.

Always give something back to the horse. The best things are release, relief, relaxation, reward or a pat on the neck. Do something to let your horse know when he's doing right.

## Communication and Control

Horsemanship is all about communication and control. You need control of the whole horse — head, neck, shoulders, rib cage, hindquarters, all the way through to his feet. And then you need to communicate so he'll understand the game you're asking him to play. He shouldn't fear it or hate it; you shouldn't have to drag him into the arena to do it. If you could do it right, I think most horses would love the sports we ask them to do.

A great barrel horse understands his job; he runs from his heart. A great cutting horse likes to cut cattle; he dares a cow to get past him. The ones that quit and run off on the ends are sometimes scared to death. Horses that have bad reactions to performance are afraid of what they're doing. Many times it's a loss of confidence and trust. They don't understand it and were probably pushed too hard and too fast to perform. A loss of confidence can be hard to regain.

*The best barrel racing horses must learn the fundamentals of the game before they can become truly competitive.*

If you can get past the fear to the understanding, then you'd have total control of your horse because he'd understand the game you're playing.

Give horses a year or two to understand your game, not 30 days. By not progressing too hard and fast, you avoid the element of fear. There are times when your horse will get a little nervous and unsure about what you're doing. Right then, stop and go back to something the horse understands. When he regains his confidence and calmness, return to the lesson and start over again.

## Learning to Learn

Allow your horse to learn. It's a time-consuming process. For example, don't try to get your horse spinning very quickly until he learns how to give to pressure, follow his nose, and place and move his feet. Just like fine wine, learning takes time. Anything that's worthwhile usually takes time. Give your horse the opportunity to learn. He didn't come into the world knowing what you want.

You train horses to learn by going through a series of basics. For example, in teaching a horse to turn around or spin,

like reiners do, first you ask for a little bend or yield, then a circle; then you get a quarter-pivot or turn. Be happy with that, recognize and reward it. Before long you're getting a half-pivot, then a three-quarter pivot; then your horse turns all the way around one time.

Horses are capable of latent learning. That means it might take a few days or weeks for something to click mentally for a horse. You might not think he understands when you're training him one day, but then the next day or in a few days, he's got it. Give the horse a chance to solve it, soak it in, to pick it up, to mentally process what it is you're trying to tell him. Some pick things up right away; others take longer. Some horses are just slower learners.

## Be Willing to Change

Be willing to change, to let go of your ego and pride. The horse doesn't have an ego or pride like a human does, which is one reason he's easy to teach. So if you find something that's not working for you, be willing to change. It doesn't matter who taught you — your dad or granddad or the world's latest champion. If you try a

*Reining horses master complicated 360-degree turnarounds one step at a time. First, they learn where to place their feet. Speed comes much later in the game after the horse fully understands the maneuver's mechanics.*

method or technique with your horse and he isn't getting it, try another approach. Read another book, watch another video, take constructive criticism, but find another approach to help your horse understand what it is you're trying to teach him. You'll know when he's confused because he'll start to show signs of nervousness and what you might take for belligerence. Actually, he just doesn't understand what you're asking of him.

**Remember:** If you can't change, then you can't grow. If you can't grow, then you can't be your best. And if you can't be your best, what else is there?

## Horseman Versus Trainer

A great horseman is a fair and patient communicator. Here's an interesting analogy when it comes to training horses. Say you measure knowledge in terms of electric volts. One trainer has 100 volts and another has only 75. But the trainer with 100 volts can communicate only 40 volts to the horse. And the trainer who has 75 volts can pass along all 75 to the horse. Which

trainer do you want riding your horse? I'd rather have the trainer with 75.

There's a difference between a great horseman and a great horse trainer. I've known a lot of horse trainers, even champions, whom I don't respect. Horses are just things to them, just objects, something they use on their way to glory. The championships are always about them, not their horses.

To me, a big part of horsemanship and horse training is trust and it's a two-way street. It's a trust I must have of my horse and he of me. In the dictionary, trust is described as faith, hope and a reliance on another. It also mentions confidence and doing things without fear or misgivings. These are all qualities I try to develop in my horses.

To trust is to believe in something. As horse people, it's easy for us to destroy the trust or belief our horses have in us. If you train through pain or fear, you destroy the trust the horse has in you. Trust, like confidence, can be gained and lost. You can't make something or somebody trust or believe in you, you can only gain this trust or respect by the way you work with or train your horse.

*In a world full of big, scary objects, a horse must have confidence in his rider that all is safe and well. Much of horsemanship and horse training depends on a trusting relationship between horse and human.*

## True Story: A Tale of Trust

*I once owned a big, beautiful buckskin gelding named K-Boy. As handsome as this horse was, I bought him cheap. He'd been abused and consequently had no trust in human beings. I was aware of these circumstances when I made the purchase, but I was sure I could help this troubled buckskin.*

*Regaining trust is always a slow process, but just the awareness of that reality makes it an easier process for me. I knew it was going to take time, and time is something I'm always willing to give a horse.*

*K-Boy responded to constant handling and riding, and the long re-schooling process began to pay off. He became a top using and ranch horse, and, in time, turned out to be my most trusted and favorite horse. Whether chasing cattle in heavy brush or working colts, K-Boy was my main mount.*

*One August, while on the trail of an outlaw Brangus bull, I tried crossing a deep, muddy slew. Low and behold, there was no bottom in this quicksand and we bogged down fast and deep. I dove from the saddle and scrambled to higher ground on the bank. Out of breath, I looked back at my buckskin partner sunk and stuck in the mud — nothing but his head and shoulders showing. But worse, he was still sinking.*

*The other cowboys offered to ride for help and even bring back a tractor. But I knew by that time it'd be too late. Cautiously, I eased my way back to my horse as my compadres shouted other ideas and instructions to help. I took hold of the reins and got after K-Boy with verbal and physical commands for all I was worth. It was now or never. You hear horsemen talk about horses with heart. Believe me, that big horse found some, and, with all his strength, powered himself and me out of that bog and up to the top of the bank to safety. To this day, I believe it was the trust between us that gave him the heart to get out of that bad situation.*

*K-Boy and I lived to ride many a mile and make many a horse track after that day. One morning, however, K-Boy didn't come up with the other geldings at feeding time. I rode down to the pasture and there he stood, grazing by himself. Upon closer examination my heart jumped, as it was easy to see his front left cannon bone broken in two. The skin was not broken, but the leg was dangling, nonetheless. I knew what I had to do. I sent one of the hands for the gun. I spent some time talking to that old horse until the inevitable had to be done. At the final moment, I looked into those big, brown eyes and even then I saw only trust.*

## Enough is Enough

How do you know when you've trained or ridden enough for a day?

Recognize when your horse is trying. Even though you might not have gotten to the point you had in mind that day, if your horse is trying, maybe that's enough for that day. Don't push it to where things become bad. You always want to end on a good note.

One thing I see people do, even at my camps and clinics, is after they learn new training techniques, they make the mistake of never stopping their training. I'll yell out to them: "When are you going to stop training on that horse?" They look at me and say, "What?"

There have to be resting spots for horses. Resting spots are extremely important to the horse, especially when you're doing things that are mentally and physically taxing to him. Learn to find a stopping spot. Drop your reins, turn loose of the horse and let him relax and catch his breath. This is part of giving something back to the horse. Rest, relief, release, relaxation, reward, a pat on the neck. Let him rest a minute or two.

You've also got to take into consideration a lot of different things. How long have you been riding the horse? What is his disposition? How hot is it outside? When you add the humidity and temperature together and they total 180, be careful. Then enough can be enough real quickly. The horse can become overheated and not be able to cool himself down. He could even die. If you get a horse too hot and too tired, he can't learn or think anymore. And if you push, the horse will become angry. You can't train an angry horse. An angry horse can't learn.

Be a great teacher to your horse. To do so, you need to be a great student of horsemanship. Teaching is the art of communication. Work on the little plateaus, the little changes, the little tries. Reward them and build upon them. Those are your building blocks.

# Goal-Setting

Set goals for yourself in horsemanship because that's the only way you'll know if your relationship with your horse is working. But come up with small ones — they're more believable and therefore achievable.

Work on reaching small plateaus, not climbing insurmountable mountains. I think a mistake that many of us make is that we ask way too much way too fast of ourselves and of our horses. We need to slow down. Take our time. Don't get in a hurry with horses.

# HERE'S HOW

## Come to Me

Teach your horse to come to you, but remember that there needs to be something in it for the horse. That something is typically relief, reward and relaxation.

Do your catching homework in a round pen. The controlled environment makes it easier on both of you. When you first do this exercise, put a halter on your horse, along with either the 12-foot lead rope, 25-foot rope or 50-foot rope.

With you in the middle, send your horse around the pen, at either a trot or lope. Make him work.

Decide on a cue that means "Come to me." It can be a whistle or a smooch or your outstretched hand, anything, but be consistent with it always. Give the cue, then reel the horse in on the rope.

Make the resting spot be with you. When your horse comes to the center, pet him, reward him for coming by letting him rest a minute. Then, drive him off again and repeat until he comes to you on the signal alone.

I've been asked about giving horses a treat, such as a carrot, sugar cube or horse treat, as a reward for coming to you. To me this is trick-training. I'm not saying it's the wrong thing to do. The problem with the treat is that a lot of horses will resent it when you don't have one. You want your horse to come to you because he wants to, not because you bribed him into it.

*1. After your horse learns to come to you on line, send him off at liberty.*

After your horse comes willingly to you on line (with lead rope or lariat), work him at liberty in the round pen. If you have to stop him, block his forward movement by heading him off, give the cue, then walk backward to the middle to draw him toward you.

From here, advance to a bigger pen or arena. Do the same thing as in the round pen, first on a line, then at liberty. Your horse should be able to make the transition nicely, but if not, go back to the round pen for more schoolwork.

*2. Allow him to make a few laps, then block his forward movement by moving toward his head.*

*3. Draw your horse to you by walking backward toward the middle of the pen, using your "come to me" cue. It can be a smooch, an outstretched hand, whatever. When he comes to you, allow him to rest and let that be his reward.*

# 5

# EQUIPMENT, TOOLS OF THE HORSEMAN'S TRADE

Good equipment is a must. As in any job, you need tools to get it done properly and efficiently. I like simple tools that are easy for the horse to understand. I don't encourage the use of gimmicks or quick-fix items, such as stud chains, tie-downs or bonnet chains. Horsemanship is an art that takes time. Effective, time-tested, simple tools are the true horseman's choice.

## Halter

A good rope halter is an essential piece of equipment, not only for restraining your horse, but also for communicating with him. With the smaller, thinner dimension of a rope halter, horses learn to give to pressure more easily and quickly and that teaches them to be light. Plus, a rope halter is one continuous piece of rope, usually made of yachting braid or climbing rope, which is some of the strongest rope made. A horse who pulls or sits back on the halter rope isn't giving to pressure. Instead, he's going against it.

I don't like nylon web or leather halters. They're both wide and lie flat against a horse's cheekbones, which

*There's no substitute for good equipment. Not only can it last a lifetime, it can also save your life.*

*A rope halter is made of one continuous piece of rope.*

horse learns to respect the rope's pull and yields to that pressure.

Whereas, with a web halter, your horse might lean into it and become heavy in your hands. You end up lugging him around, not leading him around. Also, a rope halter is light and easy for your horse to carry.

There's a correct way to tie a rope halter so your knot comes undone easily. (See "Here's How" titled "Tying a Rope Halter.") There's an eye in the rope's end. You should tie your knot below it, with the rope's tail pointing away from the horse's eye. Then, if a horse pulls back, it won't tighten so much that you can't untie it.

## Ropes

Ropes are essential pieces of equipment in my training program. I always say that if I have a rope halter, 12-foot lead rope, two 25-foot long lines and a 50-foot horse-handling lariat rope, I can work any horse, any time, anywhere.

I prefer a 12-foot long lead rope rather than the typical 8- or 9-foot variety because it allows me ample room to handle my horse.

A lead rope that's soft and pliable in your hands (like the kind made out of yachting rope or braid) is best to work with. Yachting rope is strong, has lots of life and is easy to handle. Any rope can burn your hands.

Make sure the lead rope has a good stainless-steel or brass bull snap. Cheaply made ones break under pressure, which horses put them under all the time. Ideally, the snaps should be braided on, not clamped. Clamps won't hold up when a 1,000-pound horse decides to pull back.

However, my favorite lead line ties to the halter; it doesn't snap. Because it's tied, there's no snap or device to break. (See "How to Tie a Lead Rope to a Rope Halter," page 63)

In addition to a good lead rope, I use a variety of other rope lengths to handle my horses. One of my favorites is a set of long lines or driving lines. They're 25 feet long, made of soft cotton with heavy-duty snaps on the ends. (In this case, the snaps work well because I don't use them for tying

encourages a horse to lean or lay on the halter. Also, they can break anywhere there's stitching or hardware, which is maybe 15 or 16 different places.

You don't want your halter to break. If it does break when your horse pulls back, he learns that all he has to do is sit back and he's free. If he breaks the halter enough times, it becomes a habit. A habit is the easiest thing to make and the hardest thing to break. (See "A Better Way" titled, "Curing the Pull-Back Horse.")

You can teach your horse to be light in a rope halter because its thin dimension works on pressure points on your horse's head — over his poll and nose. When you make contact with or bump your horse by tugging on the lead line, he learns to yield to the rope pressure, to be soft, light and responsive. It doesn't feel good to lay into a rope halter because the smaller dimension rope presses sharply into his skin. Your

# HERE'S HOW

**Tying a Rope Halter:** The correct way to tie a rope halter helps prevent it from overtightening.

1. Hold the rope's tail end in your right hand and the eye-loop portion in your left. Bring the tail end down through the eye loop.

2. Lift the eye-loop's knot in preparation for placing the tail end underneath the eye loop.

3. Bring the tail end underneath the loop.

4. The tail should now be on the left side of the knot.

5. Bring the tail end over the eye loop and back through the opening between the eye loop and the tail end of the rope itself.

6. A close-up of the knot you're forming. Hold the tail end in your right hand.

7. Pull the tail end to tighten and secure the knot.

8. The finished knot should look like this. Note the tail end is away from the horse's face and secured underneath the jaw piece.

*A 25-foot long cotton rope is great for round-pen work, longeing, ground driving, desensitizing and trailer loading.*

*A 50-foot lariat with a horse-handling honda is useful in many training situations.*

horses.) I use these lines for everything: longeing, desensitizing, ground driving, trailer loading and problem solving.

The 25-foot line is good for round-pen work, since most round pens are 45 to 55 feet in diameter. That allows me to be in the middle and have comfortable control of my horse, who's on the perimeter.

I don't like flat nylon longe lines because they're lightweight. I like something that has a little weight to it — that makes it easier to control the lines, put them where I want and telegraph messages to the horse.

Also, in ground driving, the 25-foot line works well when I hook up both lines to the horse's halter, rope hackamore or snaffle bit.

I also use what I call a 50-foot horse-handling lariat rope. It has a small dimension (called a scant) with an extra-soft lay (a term used to describe a rope's stiffness). Ropes are made of twisted strands of nylon or nylon-blend fibers and the amount of twist determines the stiffness of the lay.

The 50-foot rope gives me plenty of rope with which to work, whether I'm on the ground or working in the saddle from another horse. I can loop it around the horse's neck, hocks or over the head. I can even rope a foot with it.

My horse-handling rope has a horse-handling honda (a loop at the end through which the rope runs). Mine is made of metal or rawhide with a round eye from 1 to 2 inches wide, making it easy for the rope to feed through the eye or honda. That allows me to turn loose of the horse the instant I want or need to, which provides an immediate reward or release for the horse.

Even if you're not proficient at handling a rope, give it a try. It's like anything else. It feels awkward in the beginning, but the more you use it, the better you get.

## Saddle

This is personal preference and depends on what you do with your horse — such as reining, barrel racing, cutting, roping, jumping or trail riding. The main thing is that it should fit you and your horse. If either of you gets sore, then the equipment doesn't fit. An ill-fitting saddle can cause a sore back, dry spots and saddle sores on your horse's back.

Check to make sure your saddletree isn't broken. Rock the saddle from side to side. It'll twist or give from side to side if it is. Also, look for nails or screws poking through the fleece on the underside of your saddle.

The bars of the saddletree shouldn't pinch the horse, so purchase a saddle built for your horse's breed or at least the shape of his back. There are many types of trees and bars and a lengthy discussion of them is beyond the scope of this book. But a saddletree built for a narrow Arabian can be vastly different than one for a wide-bodied Quarter Horse.

When it comes to the seat length, don't buy a saddle that's too small for you. Sometimes I see people riding saddles in which they're squashed between the saddle's swells and the cantle. You need room to move when you ride, so make sure there's at least an inch or two between your seat and the saddle swells as well as the cantle. If you're unsure, seek advice from a professional saddlemaker.

Seat width is also personal preference. For myself, I prefer a narrow seat in which my legs hang down by my sides naturally, not spread apart. This style sets me close to my horse, almost as if I were riding bareback. I want to feel my horse's sides as I ride, as well as swing my legs freely, which enables me to cue easily. Too

*Craig prefers a saddle with a narrow seat and free-swinging stirrup leathers.*

*Saddles with bulkless rigging lie flat against the horse's side and allow for good leg contact.*

wide a seat spreads your legs apart, as does bulky rigging underneath your legs. This bulkiness and excess rigging can also be uncomfortable.

There are saddles with stirrup leathers that put your legs and feet too far behind your hips, which, in turn, tilts your body too far forward as you ride. It's best to test-ride a saddle before you buy to make sure it allows you to sit in a comfortable and secure position and use your legs at the same time. Also, free-swinging stirrup leathers let you use your legs more effectively to cue your horse.

There are many stirrup styles on the market. Buy the type that suits your riding discipline. For example, if you ride a cutting horse, you might prefer the traditional, narrow oxbow stirrup. But if you're a trail rider who rides cross-country for long periods, a wider, bell-shaped stirrup is more comfortable because it distributes pressure evenly along the bottom of your foot.

Rigging is what attaches the cinch to the saddle, and there are various positions for it on the saddletree. Full, seven-eighths, three-quarter, and center-fire are the traditional or standard positions, and they range from the front of a saddle (full) to almost under the rider's leg (center-fire). A full-double

saddle is rigged in the full (or front) position, combined with a back cinch.

Some saddles pull so far down in the front with their cinch rigging that the rear of the saddle sticks up. Whatever rigging you choose, make sure it pulls evenly on both sides and keeps the saddle flat, balanced and stable on the horse's back.

Although I prefer a leather latigo or tie strap, from time to time I use a nylon one, because of its pulling ease. But leather is more natural against the horse's hide and is less apt to cause galls. Unlike nylon, it also gives a little as the horse breathes and moves.

One of the best things you can do for yourself and your horse is to buy a hand-made, custom saddle from a knowledgeable saddlemaker. Many makers can construct a pretty saddle, but you want one who knows how to build a saddle that's comfortable and fits both you and your horse.

I recommend finding a saddlemaker with a reputation for quality work. The saddle will most certainly cost more than a production model, but then you always get what you pay for. Often, these makers are so busy that you'll have to wait months, even years, to get your equipment. But then it'll fit you and your horse better than a factory or production saddle that was built on an assembly line. Some good makers do have semi-custom models and many of these are just as good as the one-of-a-kind variety. A good one will last a lifetime. You can pass it on to your grandchildren. I have my grandfather's saddle, made in the 1940s, and it's still in great shape.

## Cinch

There are many choices in cinches. I like those made out of natural fibers, such as 100-percent mohair wool or mohair blend. Some of the neoprene and nylon cinches are all right for short rides. However, if I have my horse saddled for a long time, especially in hot weather, I like to use cinches made with natural fibers, which breathe and have some stretch or give to them. When a horse takes a breath, he's not restricted in his girth area by a tight cinch that has no give to it. A mohair cinch gives a little and lets air circulate as well. The neoprene and nylon cinches can get hot, and if they rub a horse long enough, they can cause galls.

Also, I don't like a narrow cinch. I prefer one that flares out like a roping cinch because when you tighten it, the pressure is distributed over a wider area. That's more comfortable for the horse.

*Tip:* When you adjust your cinch, make sure it's even on both sides of the horse's body. Don't have the cinch ring high on one side and lower on the other. Make sure the middle of the cinch is in the middle of the horse's body. Cinch rings should be evenly spaced on both of the horse's sides.

The cinch should be the proper size for the horse's heart-girth. A 30- to 32-inch cinch is a good average length that fits a lot of horses.

I find a back cinch useful in helping keep a saddle down on the horse's back. Adjust it so that it's snug against the horse if you plan on roping. Otherwise, tighten it just so the horse knows it's there. Definitely don't have it so loose it hangs down. Your horse can get it caught on something or stick his foot through it. It can be especially dangerous riding downhill. Your horse could easily run his foot through the back cinch and then you're in for the biggest wreck of your life.

## Saddle Pad and Blanket

Good saddle pads and blankets are designed to protect a horse's withers and back from too much pressure. They also should fit the horse, rather than be too thin or thick. Using two thick pads to protect your horse's back might be too much. You have to cinch the horse too tightly and that's uncomfortable for him. Because the saddle is perched on top of the thick pads, it might very well roll from side to side and not stay stationary in the middle of the horse's back. This, in turn, can cause a sore back.

Some saddle pads are actually combination blanket/pads. They combine a Navajo blanket-type material with a fleece underpad. The more natural the material that goes against the horse's skin, such as wool fleece, the better. However, some synthetic fleece (such as the type called "hospital" fleece) is good for your horse's back, just as it's good for bed-ridden hospital patients.

*Wool saddle pads or blankets have been the standard in back protection for many years.*

Natural materials are more comfortable for your horse. If he's uncomfortable or hurting somewhere, his mind isn't on you or what you're doing, but on the pain he's experiencing.

## Sore Backs

Your horse's back should have an even sweat pattern over it when you lift the saddle and saddle pad after a ride. That means there was even pressure or tension throughout the saddle's bearing surface. Look for dry spots, which have been created by undue pressure from the saddle. That means the saddle is pressing too much on that spot. In time, the horse will end up with a saddle sore, and you'll have a sore-backed horse.

One good way to check whether your horse's back is sore is to run your fingers down both sides of your horse's spine when you remove the saddle after a ride. Use a slight amount of pressure in your fingers when you do so. If your horse flinches, he might be sore.

It's amazing how much lameness can be attributed to back soreness. A horse tends to protect himself in the back area by using his legs differently, such as taking shorter strides or compensating in some way for back pain. That, in turn, causes him to become sore in his legs and feet.

Another cause of back soreness is the rider not sitting the horse correctly. For example, the rider leans one way or the other or too far forward or back, instead of sitting squarely in the middle of the horse.

## Bits and Other Communication Tools

Bits have been in use as tools of communication and control for as long as humans have ridden horses. They come in different shapes and sizes. Most bits are made of metal, mainly steel and iron. Some mouthpieces are made of copper or have copper inlays, which encourages salivation. The ones I prefer most have mouthpieces made of sweet iron, which is

*To check whether your horse's back is sore, run your fingers down both sides of his spine. If he flinches, he might be hurt in that spot.*

*The copper rollers on this D-ring snaffle encourage salivation in a horse's mouth.*

a porous steel that rusts and has a tangy taste horses like. The taste also encourages salivation, which lubricates the mouth. A moist mouth is one sign of a relaxed horse.

Bits work on feel and pressure within the horse's mouth, which include the corners, lips, tongue, palette or roof of the mouth and bars. Other pressure points are the bridge of the nose, the poll and the chin groove, which is where the curb strap or chain rests.

How the bit is designed determines which pressure points are used. Shank length and angle and the mouthpiece design dictate where and how much pressure the horse experiences.

Good horsemen agree that bits aren't designed to make a horse do something, but to guide and teach what it is we want and don't want of him.

Bits shouldn't be used as weapons or instruments of torture, but as tools of communication. Remember, the bit is only as good as the hands using it.

When it comes to communication, the three most common tools are snaffle bits, hackamores and finally, leverage bits.

## Snaffle Bit

A snaffle bit is the true training bit and typically the first bit used on a young horse. Its design is simple: a mouthpiece, usually jointed (but not always), and connected by two rings. The bit works mostly on the corners of the horse's mouth and not as much on the bars. Because it does, it allows you to have a direct feel of the horse's mouth and allows the horse to follow a simple and direct feel from your reins.

One of the beauties of the snaffle bit is that it gives you a one-to-one ratio. In other words, 1 pound of pressure in your hands equals 1 pound of pressure in the horse's mouth. The snaffle gives you a true feel of your horse in your hands.

With a snaffle bit, use a half-inch-wide leather curb strap, not a curb chain. The strap prevents you from accidentally pulling the snaffle bit through the horse's mouth.

## Hackamore/Bosal

The word "hackamore" comes from the Spanish word "jaquima," which, in turn, comes from the Arabic word "al-hakma." When the Moors conquered Spain, they did so riding their Arabian horses with an al-hakma, or loop around the animal's nose. The Spanish adopted this form of control, and it endures today in our bosals or hackamores. The word "bosal" derives from the Spanish word "bozal," which means muzzle.

The complete hackamore outfit consists of a bosal (noseband), headstall (or hanger), mecate reins (braided horsehair and lead rope) and sometimes a fiador (throatlatch).

With respect to hackamores, I'm not talking about the mechanical type, which uses metal shanks attached to a noseband. That makes it a leverage device. I'm referring to the true hackamore, which works mostly on nose and cheek pressure.

*Most snaffles are jointed in the middle, but not always. This is a typical D-ring snaffle with leather curb strap.*

training. The smaller the diameter, the more severe the bite, depending on the hackamore's construction. A hard rawhide hackamore with a small diameter would have more "bite" than one made out of soft latigo leather.

Besides traditional hackamores, I often use a rope hackamore in the early stages of training. It's useful in teaching the green horse to bend and give, saving his mouth before introduction to the snaffle bit. Rope hackamores are nosebands without heel knots. They can be made of nylon, hemp or hemp covered with soft rawhide.

In the earlier stages of training a young horse, I sometimes like to use a sidepull, a variation of the hackamore. A sidepull is a loop of leather or rope hung on a simple headstall. The reins attach to a ring braided into the headstall at the sides. This allows the rider to use direct pressure on the sides of the horse's head for control. The action is similar to a snaffle bit, although here you put pressure on the sides of the horse's cheeks and not the corners of his lips, thus

The terms "hackamore" and "bosal" are often interchanged. Both refer to nosebands. In this book, I'll refer to them as hackamores.

Most good hackamores have a rawhide core, which gives them flexibility. Hackamores made with nylon or metal cores are rigid and, therefore, they don't afford the "live feel" most good horsemen look for in a communication device.

The outside of the hackamore can be made either of braided rawhide or latigo leather and sometimes even twisted horsehair.

Parts of the hackamore include a nose button, which rests across the bridge of the horse's nose; the side buttons, which secure the headstall in place; the cheekpieces and the heel button or heel knot. The latter counterbalances the nose button and is where the reins (usually mecate) attach.

Hackamores come in a variety of sizes, anywhere from a 1/4- to 1-inch, measured at the cheekpieces. The diameter depends on the individual horse and where he is in his

*A latigo leather bosal showing the nose button, side buttons, cheekpieces and heel knot.*

*Rope hackamores are often used in the early stages of training.*

saving the mouth. The sidepull is good because it offers a direct pull, which is easy for the horse to follow and understand.

Although you can start a horse in a traditional heel-knot hackamore, it's normally used after snaffle-bit work. It helps develop a horse's refinement and headset in the transitional period before introducing the full bridle. Bridling is the final step in a horse's education. This is when the horse advances to leverage bits.

## Leverage Bits

A leverage bit employs leverage principles for communicating to and controlling the horse. This type of bit works off levers (the shanks) and a fulcrum (the mouthpiece). Simply put, the more leverage a bit produces, the more pressure the rider can apply to the horse's mouth.

Leverage bits have jointed or solid mouthpieces and shanks that come in various lengths and styles. They're always used in conjunction with curb straps or chains, which allow the bit's leverage action to take effect.

Leverage bits offer a mechanical advantage to the rider that snaffle bits don't. Here's how they work.

When the rider pulls on the bridle reins, the bit shanks (levers) move or sweep backward. When they do, the mouthpiece (fulcrum) rotates forward in the horse's mouth. As the shanks move backward, the curb strap or chain engages in the chin groove to stop the shanks' movement. The horse's mouth is thereby caught in a squeeze.

Bit severity correlates to shank length and mouthpiece-port height and design. Generally, the longer the shank (the more pulling power) and the higher the port (the more roof-palate pressure), the more severe the bit.

Bit leverage is expressed in ratios. The higher the ratio, the more pressure the bit exerts on the horse's mouth. As I mentioned earlier, the snaffle bit with its direct pull offers 1 pound of pressure for each pound of pull on the reins or a 1:1 ratio. There are various ratios with leverage bits, but typically they average 1:3 (considered moderate) to 1:7 (severe).

When I progress from a snaffle to a leverage bit, I prefer to start with a bit

*The jointed mouthpiece on this medium-shanked bit has a copper roller for salivation. Also, because of its loose-shanked construction, this bit offers independent rein action.*

## True Story: Your Life's Riding on It

*A man who attended a spring clinic at my Double Horn Ranch refused to heed my warning about a frayed cinch. He didn't want to spend the money for a new one, claiming the old one still had plenty of life! What life the cinch had left nearly cost the man his life. He ended up underneath his horse when the cinch broke a few hours later. Fortunately, I stopped his horse, and the man wasn't hurt. Needless to say, he bought a new cinch immediately, but it was after the fact. He learned a tough lesson that could have been avoided.*

*In my opinion, good equipment is an absolute must. I always say there isn't much riding on your equipment, just your life, but you make your own choice. In any craft, good equipment makes the job easier and safer.*

that's loose-jawed, loose-shanked and has a simple, jointed mouthpiece. Because of its loose or hinged construction, this style of bit maintains an independent rein action similar to a snaffle. However, it also gives me the mechanical advantage of leveraged pressure, which I use to develop refinement and lightness in the horse.

I like gently curved shanks, 5 to 7 inches in length, measured from the headstall ring to the rein ring. This style shank gives the horse a slower signal before the bit engages, allowing him more time to respond to the rein cues. A straight shank gives very little warning or signal of bit engagement, and therefore can be more severe.

In the beginning, I prefer to use curb straps to curb chains because they're milder and have some give to them.

Of course, the mildness or severity of any bit depends on the hands that use it.

## Headstalls

Headstalls come in two basic varieties: browband and split or one-ear.

Browband headstalls are aptly named because of the band across the horse's brow, connecting both sides of the cheekpieces. They also have a throatlatch strap that adjusts behind the horse's jaw, securing the headstall and preventing the horse from rubbing it off.

Split-ear headstalls have a slit in the crown piece through which the right ear goes. A one-ear headstall works the same way, but there's a sliding loop of leather or nylon for the right ear. Both these headstalls can have throatlatch straps as well. However, often they don't and that makes it easy for a horse to rub off this type of headstall.

I prefer a wide, leather headstall — 3/4 to 1-inch thick — rather than nylon because I think it's more comfortable for the horse. Also, leather is a much more natural material against the horse's skin. When it gets hot, nylon can rub or burn a horse.

The correct headstall to use with a rope hackamore or a snaffle bit is a browband headstall. Don't use a split- or one-ear headstall because if the split is on the right ear and you pick up on the left rein, the whole cheekpiece comes way back and you lose a lot of your effectiveness and control.

*Browband headstalls are the correct choice to use with D-ring snaffles and hackamores.*

Instead, use a browband headstall with a throatlatch strap and your hackamore or snaffle bit will remain stable and more effective in the horse's mouth or on his nose.

*Tip:* Make sure the buckles or hardware on the headstall don't rub or pinch your horse. Don't tighten the throatlatch to the point where your horse can't flex at the poll.

## Reins

Reins come in two basic styles: split (two separate pieces) or one continuous loop. The type I use depends on what type of bit or hackamore I have and the job at hand.

With a snaffle bit, I sometimes use mecate reins — a 22-foot piece of rope that can be made out of horsehair or synthetic material, such as nylon, parachute cord or yachting cord. The horsehair variety comes from either mane hair for a softer feel or tail hair for a coarser feel. As with hemp, both are a little prickly, which allows the horse to feel them against his neck.

The mecate is a continuous solid rein from bit ring to bit ring — 10 feet is used for the rein and the remaining 12 feet becomes a lead rope you can wrap around your saddle horn or tuck in your belt. The reins are usually attached to the snaffle bit with slobber straps, 6- or 8-inch lengths of leather. With them you get more direct pull with your snaffle bit because they're wide and a quicker release because they're heavy. The leather's weight helps the reins turn loose quickly when you release pressure, which means the rein response is instantaneous for the horse. Also, when a horse drinks out of a tank, pond or river, they get wet instead of your reins.

With a hackamore, you can use hemp (rope), cotton, nylon or a variety of different materials for reins. On traditional heel-knot hackamores, I prefer mecate-style reins made of horsehair, nylon, parachute cord or yachting braid. When I use a rope hackamore, I prefer split reins that are made of hemp. They're braided or plaited (much like a bull rope used by

PHOTO BY RICK SWAN

*Horsehair mecate reins are prickly against a horse's skin, thus helping the horse to feel the rein signal.*

*The traditional way to attach mecate reins to a snaffle bit is with slobber straps.*

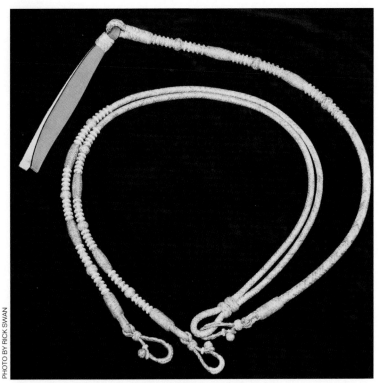

PHOTO BY RICK SWAN

*These romal reins are made of plaited rawhide.*

rodeo contestants), 3/4 to an inch wide, 7 feet long. Hemp is prickly and the horse feels it when it's laid against his neck. I like the reins to have a little bit of weight to them. That way, just like with the slobber straps, when I release them, they float down, giving the horse an instantaneous response.

Split reins are commonly used with sidepulls, snaffles and shanked bits. They consist of two separate lengths of leather, about 7 to 8 feet long, made out of a full cowhide, not split hide. A full hide is thicker and therefore stronger. They can come in different widths. Choose reins that are comfortable for your hands to hold.

As with mecate reins, romal reins also form a continuous loop from bit ring to bit ring, with a romal, or long strap, attached to the center of the reins. There's a popper (wide piece of leather) on the end of the romal that a rider can use to encourage his horse or to get his horse's attention. This type of rein was developed by the Californios or vaqueros, who used them with spade and half-breed bits

on their finished bridle horses. They're meant for more advanced riding, when a rider can pick up the reins in one hand and guide his horse with minimal effort.

Typically, romal reins are made of braided rawhide; the more strands of leather used and the tighter the braid, the more expensive the reins. Often, there are braided knots or silver barrel ferrules in the reins design so a horse can feel them when the reins are laid against his neck, and they also add more weight to the reins. Sometimes there are bit chains attached from the bit rings to the end of the reins to add more weight and balance to the outfit.

## Protective Boots

If you choose to advance your horse's training to include high-performance maneuvers, such as sliding stops, turn-arounds and rollbacks, you must protect your horse's legs. It's hard for a horse to continue working when he's in pain. If he turns hard and steps on his own feet, hits his knees and cannon bones, or he stops hard and burns his fetlocks, he won't want to do it anymore.

Splint boots and bell boots for front legs and skid boots for hind legs are great pieces of equipment for horses, especially

*Splint boots protect your horse's front legs during performance events.*

*Skid boots are a must in sports that require horses to stop hard.*

*Bell boots offer protection to a horse's pasterns and coronary bands.*

performance horses. They're made of leather and synthetic materials, and usually fasten with Velcro®.

Wraps, often called "standing" or "polo" wraps, are another form of protection and were what horsemen typically used until protective boots came along. They're long pieces of felt or cotton, about 3 inches wide, designed to wrap around a horse's cannon bones. Many people, especially English riders and racehorse trainers, still prefer them.

I use them only for wrapping wounds or hauling horses. My personal opinion is that protective boots are easier to put on the horse and offer more protection and support.

## Hobbles

I think every horse ought to be hobble-broke. (See Chapter 11, "Hobble-Breaking.") Hobbles teach horses to give and yield to pressure all the way down to their feet, to stand ground-tied and not to panic should they get tangled in wire or a hay net. Instead of fighting, they learn to stay calm and not move until someone tends to them. That sure helps prevent horses from getting injured.

I've found that nylon, rawhide or leather hobbles always gall horses' legs when they're not used to being restrained this way. So I designed training hobbles that are made of soft, wide (4 to 6 inches), braided cotton. They don't burn or gall horses, and, because cotton has a slight give to it, horses don't feel as trapped. I have a front-leg hobble and a side-line hobble that attaches a front leg and corresponding hind leg together.

Once a horse learns his lesson in the training hobbles, then I think it's okay to use the more traditional materials, such as nylon, leather or rawhide.

## Spurs

I've heard people refer to spurs as inhumane; but as with any piece of equipment, they're only as good as the person using them.

Using spurs properly allows you to be more precise and lighter with your horse and your horse to be more responsive. They let you communicate with your horse in a subtle way. But you must learn to use spurs correctly. Spurs are for pressing, pushing and squeezing, not for stabbing and jabbing.

There are times when I bump a horse with a spur if he's tuning me out or quitting me, but generally I just push or press with them to cue my horse.

I like to use a dull, round rowel that I can roll up or press on the horse's side. Sharp, pointy spurs should be used only by educated horsemen who know how to apply light pressure for instantaneous response.

# A BETTER WAY

## Curing the Pull-back Horse

A horse sitting back when tied is a horse not yielding to pressure, in other words, not giving to the feel of the halter while standing tied. Here's one effective method to remedy this problem.

1. Put your horse in the round pen. Use a rope halter on your horse and snap on a 25-foot long line. Loop (don't tie) the long line around a post or one of the highest rails of the pen. Note that this round pen should be a permanent fixture with sturdy posts cemented in the ground. Portable panels can be unsafe for this procedure.

2. Encourage your horse to sit back by flagging or using any fast movement to spook him.

3. The horse will go backward expecting to hit the end of the rope. Since he's not tied, there's no end and he's got 25 feet to go back.

4. Wherever he stops, reel him back to his original, simulated tied position near the post or rail.

5. Pet and reassure your horse.

6. Spook him again and continue this procedure until he doesn't spook or sit back anymore.

The philosophy is that the wrong thing (sitting back) is work and the right thing (standing tied quietly) is relief. Be sure to work both sides of your horse. Be patient and go slowly. You might have to repeat this procedure during several sessions.

Be sure that when you use spurs you know your feet position. You don't want to accidentally spur your horse at the wrong time. If you're short-legged, you probably need short-shanked spurs. If you have long legs, you might need longer-shanked or gooseneck-shanked spurs that allow you to find your horse's sides.

## Riding Boots

Cowboy or western boots with leather soles and riding heels are the safest footwear for riding. (English riders use knee-high leather riding boots with heels.) Good riding heels prevent your boots from slipping through the stirrups. Also, leather doesn't grip, so that if you ever have to get off a horse quickly, you can get your feet out of the stirrups easily.

Flat-soled shoes, tennis shoes and even boots with a synthetic composite or rubber soles can be dangerous. With a heel-less shoe, your foot can slip through the stirrup and cause you to get hung up. Rubberized soles are "grabby" and won't let go of the stirrup. With this type of footwear on your feet, you might not be able to get out of the saddle should you get in trouble on your horse.

## Flag

The flag is a great tool for desensitizing or "sacking out" a horse, as well as for creating energy for forward movement. It's nothing more than a long stick, about 4 to 8 feet long, with a plastic sack or bright cloth attached at one end. I use what I call a "swagger stick," which has a little loop at its end where you can tie a flag.

Some horses are really bothered by the noise and flutter of the flag, so be careful how you present it to your horse. Introduce it carefully and slowly, allowing your horse to become comfortable with it. Rub it all over his body and legs until he stands relaxed and uncaring. Don't force the flag on your horse. If it spooks him, stop, take it away, then start again.

*Boots with heels and leather soles make riding safer. Also pictured are short-shanked spurs.*

## How to Tie a Lead Rope to a Rope Halter

1. Run the end of the lead rope up through the halter ring loop.

2. Place the end of the lead rope over the top of the loop, directly underneath the knot (sometimes called a "fiador" knot).

3. Next, run the end underneath the loop, out through the middle and over the long length of lead rope.

4. Pull the short end taut and you've got an unbreakable piece of equipment.

*"Green on green
makes black and blue."*

# 6

# SELECTING THE RIGHT HORSE

I think it's important in any relationship, whether it's business, marriage or buying a new horse, that you have the right partner. When you select a horse for yourself, take your time, don't get in a hurry. It's like buying a car. You wouldn't run out and buy the first one you drive. You'd test-drive lots of them. Be willing to search and find the best horse for yourself. If you're inexperienced, get a professional or experienced horseperson to go with you and help.

A lot depends on what you want to do with the horse. Do you want a good trail horse or do you want a show-ring performance horse? Endeavor to find a horse that meets your goals.

Recognize what your goals are, where you're headed, what you're going to do with this horse. It's not a bad idea to write down what you're looking for. And, of course, you need to stay within your budget. You might want to have a veterinarian perform a pre-purchase exam to make sure the horse is sound, especially if you intend to spend a lot of money for the horse.

Be truthful with yourself. There's nothing wrong with being a green or novice rider. But be smart and find a horse that fits you. The worst chemistry is a green rider on a green horse. That's not going to work. It's a disaster waiting to happen. Remember, green on green makes black and blue.

If you're just starting out in the horse world, an older, experienced, gentle horse is what you need. That kind of horse will teach you, and you'll have lots of fun.

There are many things to look for in a horse, and a lot of it is a matter of personal preference. When you look at a horse

*Horses are individuals, just as people are, with distinctive personalities, quirks and character traits. Select the horse that best fits your personality and riding needs.*

seriously, go back to see him more than one time. You might even show up unexpectedly. Watch the way the horse is saddled and unsaddled and how he takes to being handled in general. You can watch him at liberty in a round pen or an arena. Make sure he's everything you want him to be. But remember, pretty is as pretty does.

## Buyer Beware

When checking out a prospective horse, here are some things to watch for right off the bat. They're red flags, things you should notice and consider before plunking down any hard cash.

Does the horse lead you instead of the other way around? Does he respect your personal space, or does he walk all over you? Horses that do this have no respect for people and probably won't ride much better either.

Watch the horse's attitude toward people. He might not like people. When you approach him, he should face you, not turn his hindquarters to you out of disrespect. Or he might pick his head straight up, pin his ears and not want to come to you. That might mean he's lost his confidence somewhere along the way, and he's wary about people. Earning his trust could be a long and arduous task.

When you mount the horse, look at his ears. Are they constantly pinned back on his head? That's the sign of an angry or resentful horse. Is his tail constantly swishing in agitation? He's not happy to be ridden. Does he ever relax? Is he in a hurry to leave? Do you have to hold him to keep him from leaving? A horse's first instinct in a time of trouble is to run. If your prospective horse always seems to be in a hurry when you're riding him, this can be trouble, and you might end up "going for a ride." If you pick up on the bit and his head goes straight up, he's nervous about what's about to happen. If you lay your legs against his side, even gently, does he resent it? Or does he take off like a bullet?

Also, watch out for barn- and herd-sour horses. A horse that doesn't want to leave his buddies or the barn area is trouble on the hoof and you don't need any part of that.

If you find a horse with a big engine, a lot of go, a lot of spirit, that's his personality; he'll always be that way. There's nothing wrong with that, just make sure you can control it.

## Where to Buy a Horse

One of the best ways to find a horse for yourself is to locate a reputable horse trainer in your area and have him or her help you. They might not have a horse that fits you, but they can recommend where else to look. Look out for so-called horse traders. Some are good, but many don't have the best reputations for being honest. They're only in it for the money and not for you.

Also stay away from horses that have been sold many times. If they've gone through that many hands, there's probably something wrong with them. It might not be obvious, but it'll surface in time.

Auctions are a different ballgame. They're quick sales, and often you don't know what you're getting. If you do go to an auction, go to one that has a reputation for good management and selling honest, solid, horseflesh. The typical monthly horse sale at an auction barn probably is something to avoid. You just don't know what you're getting into there, especially if you're inexperienced.

If you go to a reputable sale, get there early, go back to the stalls, check out all the horses and maybe even get a chance to ride the one you're looking at. At least be able to get into the stall and handle that horse. See what his general attitude is about people. Have the horse trotted away and back to you to see if he's sound. Most lameness shows up at a trot. Be ahead of the game by checking out the horses ahead of time. Don't wait till the moment of the auction because you won't get a chance to take a hard look at the sales horses. There are all sorts of auction trade tricks to make a horse look like something it's not.

# A BETTER WAY

## Test Ride

When checking out a horse to buy, have the owner ride the horse for you first. Ask the owner to put the horse through his paces. If you're buying a performance horse, make sure he can perform the tasks required. If you're looking for a solid trail mount, have the owner take him out on the trail first as you ride along on another horse. Watch how the prospective horse handles trail obstacles.

After you're satisfied that the horse can perform properly, either in the arena or on the trail, test-ride him yourself. Have an experienced friend or professional horseperson watch you and accept their critique.

Don't be afraid to return for a second look after you've had time to think about the horse and whether or not the animal will fit your riding needs. Hindsight is 20-20. Foresight is priceless.

*Take any horse you're considering buying for a test ride to make sure you get along with the horse and that it performs up to your expectations.*

Your best opportunity is to buy a horse privately. That way you can return and look several times. And, of course, with a private sale you have a better opportunity and time for a thorough veterinary pre-purchase exam. Most people really won't give you any kind of guarantee. But if you can come back and ride the horse again and again, you'll get a pretty good feel for the kind of horse he is and won't need that guarantee.

Don't forget that one of the most important things is safety. You want to be safe. You want your husband or wife to be safe, and you want your children to be safe. So after you determine that the horse you're looking to buy is sound and he's the horse he's supposed to be, make sure that he's gentle. For some reason, people think that if a horse is gentle, they won't get a good ride. They think he won't move out, but that's wrong.

*If you're a novice or green rider, one of the best ways to buy a horse is with the help and advice of an experienced horseperson.*

I'm always looking for a gentle horse. Just because a horse is gentle doesn't mean he won't move out and want to go someplace. Realize that there's always risk around any horse, even an older, gentle one.

## Buy Right

As far as price goes, try to buy right. I know that in the cattle business, we'd always say: "You make money when you buy, not when you sell." In other words, make sure the horse you're buying is worth the money, and that you could probably sell him at a profit later if you had to.

After you buy the horse, you need to work on yourself to develop a relationship between you and your new horse. You might need to take lessons, go to clinics, watch videos, read books or magazines to become educated and hone your horsemanship skills. It takes time to develop a good relationship.

## The Wrong Horse

There'll be times, though, when you find yourself stuck with the wrong horse. Despite all your efforts, you just might not have picked a good match for yourself. Don't

be afraid to sell the horse. You didn't marry him and don't have to keep him forever. If the horse gets you into trouble or you feel afraid riding him, get rid of him. Owning and riding the horse should be fun for you.

Check out the tests in the "Here's How" (below) "Basic Tests for a Sale Horse;" they list what to look for in a well-broke horse. A good horse should be able to pass these as a minimum. These are the basics and all horses should have this solid foundation in order to be considered good saddle mounts. As you get more experienced, you'll recognize what a good horse is and that's one that's relaxed and confident around people and when he's ridden. He relates to man well and accepts training well. Stay away from horses that seem nervous, frightened, unsure or overly spirited. Don't look for tough horses with problems. I'm not saying some of those problems can't be fixed, but is it worth your time and effort? A good horse takes time to make, and like anything else, you get what you pay for.

## HERE'S HOW

### Basic Tests for a Sale Horse

A prospective purchase should be able to pass the following tests:

1. Get caught easily.

2. Accept halter well.

3. Stand tied.

4. Have feet handled.

5. Lead well.

6. Stand still while being saddled.

7. Accept bit willingly and unbridle willingly.

8. Stand still while being mounted.

9. Longe, in a circle and over some obstacles, such as a small jump, or through a gate.

10. Trailer load.

11. Walk, trot, lope and back reasonably well. Doesn't have to be a big stopper like a reiner, but must respond to basic cues.

12. Be level-headed — physically, mentally and emotionally.

# True Story: A Perfect Match

*No one ever forgets their first horse and I certainly remember mine. He was a brown gelding named Mac, at least 20 years old. I don't think Mac had any papers and neither he nor I cared one bit.*

*In the shade of the huge, old oak trees on the ranch in Cat Spring, Texas, where I grew up, Mac and I spent many an hour on many an imaginary cowboy adventure. My brothers, Doug and Bruce, and sister Francis rode Mac bareback; he'd hold all four of us at one time. He put up with us with a kindness and understanding that I'll never forget.*

*I can remember riding Mac, my feet going 90 miles an hour, trying to get that old horse to move. He'd go anywhere I wanted to, but only in a steadfast walk. As a confident 5-year-old boy, with visions of Roy Rogers and Trigger in a dead run after the bad guys, I regarded that slow walk with more than a little frustration.*

*However, when there was real ranch work to be done, the ranch foreman, C.P. Hamer, or one of the ranch hands would hunt up Mac. I can remember one of the cowboys pulling my small saddle off Mac's back and throwing his big rig on the brown gelding, saying, "Craig, we need to have Mac today. We're working cattle." The cowboy would swing easily into the saddle and, to my amazement, would move right off into a lope. Mac would work all day, roping, cutting and sorting. At the end of the day, the hand would bring Mac back to me. Crawling back in the saddle, I just knew Mac now would surely be ready to go. I'd get my feet going 90 miles an hour again, and old Mac would move off in his usual slow walk.*

*As I look back, I realize what a great old horse Mac was. How patient and kind his horse soul must have been. He knew that I didn't know. He took care of me and my brothers and sister. He made riding safe for all of us. He was worth his weight in gold. Old Mac was part of the family, never sold, and died on the ranch. He's indelibly branded in my memory. He's standing under the big oak trees tied to the hitching rail with a small saddle cinched to his back, waiting for a little cowboy with understanding and gentleness in those big, brown eyes.*

*The moral of the story: Get a horse that fits you, your level of experience, needs and skills. Often I hear about folks buying a young horse for a child so they can grow up and learn together. Both the horse and rider know nothing and that's bad chemistry.*

*If you buy a horse through an auction, make sure it's a reputable one. The horse sales associated with major performance events are usually good bets for good horseflesh, although the prices might be a bit steep. One of the most risky places to shop a horse is at the local, weekend sale barn. You can never be confident of what's going through the ring.*

# 7

# EQUITATION, DEVELOPING A GOOD SEAT

Riding properly is a matter of developing good habits. Good equitation techniques are important whatever you do, from the simplest tasks to the most advanced maneuvers. No matter if you're catching your horse, mounting him, riding the trails, working cattle, jumping a fence or spinning a hole in the ground, your skills dictate your level of horsemanship.

Great horsemen are made, not born. Like any craft, horsemanship must be worked at. It's your level of desire, determination and dedication that counts.

Study the methods and exercises in this chapter to build a solid foundation for your horsemanship. How far you take it will be up to you.

## Mounting

I'm often asked, "What do you do about a horse that moves around when you get on?" My answer always is, "Don't get on." He learns to move the second you put your foot in the stirrup.

You can do several things right off the bat. You can longe the horse around you with your reins. In other words, make the wrong thing hard. Make him work if he wants to move around. He'll get tired of the small circles soon enough and stand still. Then try to mount again.

Or pick up on the left rein and bend your horse toward you, thus moving the hindquarters away. He ends up walking his

*Sitting relaxed and in rhythm with your horse are the hallmarks of a good seat.*

**71**

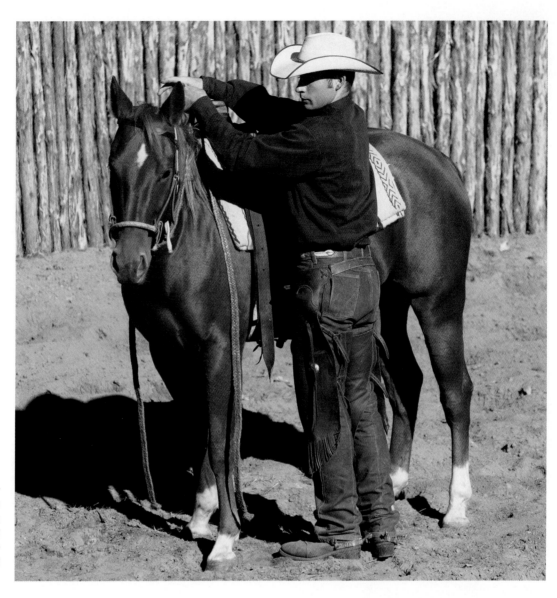

*To prevent your horse from moving, shorten your left rein and bring your horse's head toward you.*

hind end around his front end while you're on the ground. Again, you're making the wrong thing hard work. When he stops, try mounting again.

If your horse moves, grab your saddle horn and rock it back and forth hard. That forces your horse to stop, spread his legs and balance himself on the ground.

To mount, face forward toward the horse's head. Put the toe of your left boot in the stirrup, hold your left rein short enough (but not making contact) to have control over your horse should he walk off. Hold some mane in between your fingers. Grab the swell of the saddle with your right hand and pull yourself up. Swing your right leg over

the horse's hindquarters and the cantle and sit down softly on your horse's back.

If your horse attempts to walk as you're mounting, reach over and grab your right rein to stop him. Release when he stops moving.

Remember that you're the most vulnerable on any horse when you mount and dismount, so don't dilly-dally. Get the job done quickly and efficiently with little fuss and certainly no clumsiness.

Once you sit down, don't allow your horse to walk off without you asking him to. If he does, stop him and back him a step or two. Backing, in this case, is a form of discipline and helps your horse relate to you. Make him wait for a minute or two for your

1. To mount, face toward your horse's head, put the reins in your left hand and grab some mane hair. Put your left toe in the stirrup and grasp the opposite swell on your saddle.

2. Pull yourself up straight over the horse.

3. Swing your right leg over the horse's hindquarters, being careful not to bump or spur them.

4. Sit down in the saddle softly and insert your right foot in the stirrup.

1. To dismount, remove your right foot from the stirrup, lean far enough over that your horse sees you in his left eye, so he knows you're there and about to get off.

2. Swing your right leg over the saddle and horse's hindquarters, taking care not to bump or spur them.

3. Step down toward your horse's left shoulder and remove your left toe from the stirrup.

command to move forward. That creates a good habit.

Also, be careful not to inadvertently nudge your horse with your boot or spurs as you mount. That would give him conflicting signals.

## Dismount

To dismount, get prepared and do the reverse of mounting. Make sure your horse is stopped. Put your reins in your left hand if you're getting off on the left and grab a little mane with your left hand. Remove your right boot from the right stirrup and place the toe of your left boot squarely in the middle of the left stirrup. That way if your horse buggers off, you can get out of there quickly. Wiggle around in the saddle; let your horse know you're about to get off. Lean down far enough so that your horse can see you in his left eye. He knows you're coming. Then, quickly swing your right leg over the cantle and horse's hindquarters (without bumping them) and step down toward the horse's shoulder, where you can't get kicked or run over. Take your left boot out of the stirrup. Then pet your horse.

Practice getting on and off the right side as well as the left. A good horseman can mount on either side, and someday you'll find a situation in which you have to. You might be on a mountain trail somewhere where the only possibility is mounting or dismounting on the right. You certainly don't want your horse to be scared because it's the first time you've tried it. So practice at home and accustom your horse to your getting on and off both sides.

## Seat Exercises

Here's a series of exercises you can do to improve your seat and balance in the saddle. You assume different positions that help you develop a oneness with your horse and acquire what's known as a "good seat."

When you're sitting correctly on a horse, there should be a straight line from your ear, to the middle of your shoulder, to the hip and down to your heel. Your legs shouldn't be too far forward or back, but in alignment with your body. They should hang comfortably around your horse, not stiff and stuck out away from his body. Your knees should rest against your horse. Let your legs fall in a natural position, often described as "sitting in a chair." Only then are you able to use your legs, one of the best aids you have and one of the least used, I think.

These exercises can be done at a walk, trot and canter and either inside or outside an arena, but I think they're best learned in a 50- or 60-foot round corral. In the beginning, as you're learning, use your saddle; later you can do them riding bareback, as well. Bareback riding really helps develop your strength, confidence and balance. (See Chapter 8, "Bareback Riding.")

Start with a helper in the middle of the pen who makes sure your horse moves forward and along the rail. It's as if he or

*For a correct seat, sit in the saddle so there's a straight line from your ears through your shoulders, hips and heels.*

she were longing the horse on an imaginary longe line. In time, you should be able to perform these exercises without help, but in the beginning it's beneficial to have an assistant.

## Seat-Correction Exercise

You won't use your reins for the seat-correction exercise. Tie them in a knot (say, around the saddle horn or in a keeper) so they won't fall to the ground, but have them handy if you feel your horse getting out of control. However, don't tie the reins so short that they contact your horse. They should be loose, even floating. If your horse extends himself, you don't want him to bump into the bit.

Ride around the pen to the left. Walk at first and work up to a trot and canter. Be comfortable with this exercise before continuing with the others. Put your left hand behind you and hold the saddle's cantle and your right hand on the saddle horn. Literally pull yourself down to where you have a very secure feeling — that oneness where you feel really connected to your horse.

When your horse trots or canters, you shouldn't bounce in the saddle. To do this exercise, learn to use your legs and your back, the last 6 inches of your spine. Move with your horse's movement; feel it.

When traveling to the left, you might have a tendency to lean to the inside or drop your left shoulder. Instead, sit up straight. Pretend there's a carpenter's level on your back. The bubble should stay right in the middle. When you lean, your horse tends to lean in the same direction and drops his shoulder. He travels crooked and is unbalanced.

If you find yourself with a strong tendency to lean to the inside, try looking to the outside. That actually picks up your shoulder.

Any time you feel out of control during the following seat exercises, immediately return to the seat-correction position. That way you can right yourself and regain control.

*In the seat correction exercise, you ride without reins. Knot your reins around the saddle horn loosely so there's no contact with the horse's mouth. If you're going to the left, hold the cantle with your left hand and the saddle horn with the right. Reverse your hands going to the right. Literally pull yourself down on the saddle as your horse walks, trots and canters around the pen.*

# Crossed-Arms Exercise

In the crossed-arms exercise, you don't use your hands for balance or support in the saddle. With your legs straight down underneath you, wrapped around your horse with a "soft hug" so you're one with your horse, cross your arms on your chest. Sink your weight into your stirrups to help you sit deep on your horse.

Walk, trot and eventually canter using just your seat bones and legs to keep you secure in your saddle. Don't sit stiffly. You'll need to use your back and spine in rhythm to move with your horse.

In a left-lead canter, you'll feel your left leg slightly forward and your right leg slightly back. In a right lead, you'll feel your right leg slightly forward and your left leg slightly back. Your body is moving in rhythm and in time with the horse's corresponding lead.

*Cross your arms on your chest and feel the rhythm of the horse underneath you.*

# Arms-Out Exercise

Next, stick your arms straight out to your sides. Find yourself flowing with your horse's movement. This excellent exercise helps you find your balance on a horse. A word of caution: Some horses might spook at the sudden thrusting of arms into their line of sight. If it spooks your horse, stop and slowly extend your arms until he can accept them out to the sides.

Most people balance themselves on the reins, which in reality is balancing on the horse's head and mouth. That destroys a horse's rein responses, and you'll lose the soft feel you tried so hard to develop in your horse's mouth. In all these no-rein exercises, you'll have to balance with your body, seat and legs.

Often in this exercise, people lean forward. Don't get your upper body over your horse's withers, unless you're riding uphill, jumping, racing or roping. When you tip forward, you encourage your horse to speed up. Don't sit back either. Simply sit up straight in a natural position.

*Place your arms out to your sides, but be careful when you do. Some horses spook at the sudden movement. Bring your arms out slowly to accustom your horse to the sight.*

With your arms outstretched, twist your torso right, then left.

Dropping your stirrups and learning to ride "by the seat of your pants" help you to become a better rider.

## Twist Exercise

Once the arms-out position is comfortable, add a little twist to it. Twist your spine right and then left. Look over your right and left shoulders. You also can cross your arms on your chest and perform this exercise. It really loosens your torso and helps with any stiffness in your body.

## No-Stirrups Exercise

If you find yourself still bouncing too much, kick your feet out of your stirrups. You'll really have to use your seat and legs to sit down on your horse. You'll have no choice. Do this exercise even if you aren't bouncing around in the saddle a lot. It's a great balancing act and leg-strengthener.

### True Story: Tough Teacher

*A regular rider at one of my working clinics began taking his horse and sound riding practices for granted. Knowing better, he omitted any warm-up and foolishly mounted an extremely fresh horse.*

*When the horse became excited and went into a fast gallop, instead of using proper riding aids (hands, seat and legs), this hapless rider froze. When he stiffened, he became unbalanced and before he knew it, he was underneath his horse. The fall broke his leg.*

*There's really no excuse for careless riding. This was an incident that could've easily been avoided with proper preparation. The rider learned a hard lesson. Experience can sometimes be a tough teacher.*

Safety is a key ingredient when riding and is always first, so make sure you're safe and won't fall off when you take your feet out of the stirrups. Riding without stirrups teaches you to use your legs as much or more than anything else. Maintain quiet contact with your legs and use a soft touch; that's why I call it a "hug." Your thighs, knees and calves should be against your horse.

When I say leg, I don't mean feet. Use your feet as aids in turning or increasing speed only as needed.

## Close-Your-Eyes Exercise

The ultimate is to perform any of these exercises with your eyes closed. When you close your eyes, you really have to feel your horse physically, mentally and emotionally. You won't have your sight to depend on, and you'll have to learn to feel your horse. This is a terrific confidence-builder.

All these exercises help you to become more loose, limber, balanced and relaxed on your horse.

As a finale to the exercises, stop your horse without using your reins. Sit down and quit riding and see if you can't get your horse to follow that suggestion. Melt down in your saddle and say "whoa." Ninety percent of the horses I've seen do these exercises stop beautifully.

# HERE'S HOW

## Correct Way to Hold Reins

Here's the way to hold split and romal reins.

When riding young horses or those in snaffle bits, it's practical to ride two-handed. Cross the split reins over the horse's mane, hold them in your hands with your thumbs up.

For split reins, hold them in one hand, typically your left, and put your index finger between them.

Correctly hold romal reins by grasping the reins with your fingers in your left hand, thumb up, in front of the saddle horn. Hold the romal with your free hand.

# A BETTER WAY

## Smart Riding

Many horse owners claim their horses buck every morning. Generally, the problem is that the horse is just fresh and feels good. The solution is simple. Warm up your horse by moving him around in both directions at a consistent gait either in the round pen or on a longe line. Spend some time moving your horse in both directions. Put your horse to work in one direction at a time. Move him as many as 10 to 20 times before changing directions.

This simple approach takes the fresh and the fear out of your horse, which allows him to relax. This process protects you and your horse. It's no good if either of you gets hurt.

When a horse turns loose mentally, he relaxes physically and, when he relaxes physically, he turns loose mentally. This common sense is what I call "smart riding" and it complements one of my favorite horsemanship philosophies, "Smart riding is making sure you can ride again tomorrow."

# 8

# BAREBACK
# RIDING

If you can sit a horse well at all gaits bareback, then you're a good rider. Riding bareback teaches you to use your legs, creates exceptional balance and feel, and it's also fun. Frankly, it teaches you to ride!

Sitting competently while bareback is only learned by actually doing it. The easiest way to learn is on a gentle horse in a safe place so you have control and can build confidence. A round pen is about as safe a place as you can get.

It's also helpful to have an assistant or ground person to help you. Put a halter and lead rope on your horse and have your helper handle the rope from the middle of the pen. If possible, have two helpers — one on either side of the horse — to catch you if you fall as you mount and/or dismount.

## Mounting Bareback

There are several ways to mount bareback. One simple way is to stand on a 5-gallon bucket or mounting block to give yourself a lift.

Another method is to have a ground person help you. To mount on the horse's left, stand next to your horse's left shoulder and bend your left knee. Have your helper hoist you up by grabbing your left leg by the shinbone and boosting you straight up. Grab hold of your horse's mane for extra support and lift or pull your way up.

A third way is to swing or jump up without any help. This is the most difficult, but well worth knowing how. Put both

*Riding bareback helps a
rider develop a good seat.*

**81**

*One way to mount is to stand on a 5-gallon bucket.*

*You can have a helper lift you up by holding your left leg.*

hands in your horse's mane and hold on to the lead rope. Stand near your horse's left shoulder, facing your horse's hindquarters. Now, turn your body to the right and with what can best be described as a running motion take a giant leap, pushing off the ground with both legs. Swing your right leg over your horse's back. Literally pull yourself up on the horse's back. It's best not to use spurs when learning how to do this.

There's a second version: Do everything the same except instead of swinging your leg over in a giant leap, jump up and lay the torso of your body on your horse's back. Then, swing your leg over and sit up straight.

Both ways take lots of practice and can be particularly difficult with tall horses.

*There are two ways to mount unassisted: 1/ Grab some mane and take a swinging leap or…*

*…jump straight up and lay your torso over the horse's back.*

**83**

To mount from a fence, teach your horse to move right and left around you by tapping his shoulders with your swagger stick.

## Mounting from a Fence

One keen way to mount is to teach your horse to pick you up off a fence. This can be done riding bareback or with the saddle. As your horse becomes good at this procedure, you can use anything to stand or sit on — a large rock or trailer or truck fender, anything. But for teaching purposes, use a fence rail. Just make sure it's stout enough to hold your weight. Some panel fences are flimsy, so use good judgment in what you step on.

You'll need a longe whip or what I call a swagger stick as an extension of your arm. Put a halter and lead rope on your horse. Sit on the top rail of an arena or round-pen fence and longe your horse in each direction.

Use your stick to ask your horse to move to the right or left. He should follow these instructions from your earlier lessons with the flag and ropes. If you want him to move closer to the fence to your left, extend your stick with or without the flag on it and shake it or tap your horse slightly on his right side to encourage him to move to the left. When he takes a step, stop shaking or tapping. Let that be his reward and allow him to dwell on that for a moment, then begin again. Keep shaking or tapping until he comes alongside the fence. The only real resting spot for your horse should be parallel to the fence, where it's easy for you to mount.

When your horse is in good position for mounting, rub the top of his back with your boot or hand, just to make sure he isn't going to spook. Your horse should know you're up there. It shouldn't come as a surprise to him.

*There's a rider's groove or pocket right behind the horse's withers.*

Remember that you're in the same position a predator would be in to pounce. Don't let your horse's prey-animal instinct come out. Help him through it before it surfaces.

When your horse accepts your presence, kneel down on his back with one knee, still holding the fence rail should you need an emergency escape. Then sit down gently on his back.

Don't ride off immediately. Wait there a moment. Teaching your horse to wait on you is invaluable throughout your training. He learns patience and to wait for your commands.

In no time, your horse will understand what you want when you climb on top of a fence. Shake the lead rope or your reins and he'll sidle right over to the fence to pick you up.

## A BETTER WAY

### Exit Strategy

In learning to ride bareback, safety is the most important thing. Occasionally you might become unbalanced and fall off. Instead of being at the mercy of your horse, make an exit or move that keeps you out of harm's way. As a young cowboy, I learned the following maneuver from riding bulls for 20 years, and it saved me countless times.

It's basically a flying dismount. For example, if you lean to the right and find yourself past the point of no return, make a big move to throw your left leg over the horse's neck and your body away from the horse. The idea is to land on your feet or on your hands and knees, face-down. If you have a lot of momentum as you hit the ground, simply roll away from the horse. This prevents you from getting stepped on or from being haphazardly thrown in a bad position.

*Lie down slowly on your horse's back with your head resting on his hindquarters. Relax there.*

## Bareback Exercises

Once on your horse bareback, relax and get a feel of him and for him. Sit in the correct spot behind his withers. There's a groove or pocket where your seat and legs fit best. It's the most natural place to establish your balance. Even though every horse's back is different, you should have no trouble finding this secure spot. Some horses are more comfortable to sit than others. That can't be helped. You'll have to adjust to fit your horse's conformation.

There's a series of exercises you can do to become comfortable on your horse. It helps if there's a ground person to handle your horse and catch you if you fall.

Lean back slowly and lie down on your horse's back. Turn loose and relax, just as if you were on your couch at home. If your horse spooks and you don't have a ground person, roll off one way or the other.

*Sit up and lean forward to hug your horse around his neck.*

Obviously, it's best to have a good, gentle horse on which to practice. Most well-broke horses won't mind these exercises.

Sit back up. Now lean forward and hug your horse's neck with both arms. Next, swing your right leg over your horse's neck so you're sitting sideways on the left side of your horse. This really helps your agility and balance.

Next, swing the left leg over and sit backward on your horse. Lie down on your horse again; this time your head rests on the crest of his neck. Relax.

Sit back up and swing your right leg over your horse's rump. This positions you sideways on the right side of your horse.

Now reverse the entire procedure. Swing your right leg over your horse's rump and you'll be sitting backward again. Continue on around as above.

In no time, you'll become more comfortable on a horse's back and, as an added benefit,

*Sit up once again. Lift your right leg over your horse's neck. You'll find yourself sitting sideways on your horse's left side.*

*Swing your left leg over your horse's rump.*

**87**

# HERE'S HOW

## Hide on Hide

One useful suggestion for a better seat is to wear leather chaps or chinks while riding bareback. Leather against your horse's hide not only protects you, but also gives you a more secure feeling as you ride.

Personally, I never get on a horse without putting on my chaps or chinks. These traditional leg coverings create a closer contact between me and my horse, whether I ride bareback or in the saddle.

*You're now sitting backward on your horse.*

*Lie down on the crest of your horse's neck.*

your horse will become more gentle and accepting of your movements and the feel of you on him. For the first time, you'll literally feel your horse under you. You'll feel a living creature; not a saddle — a horse. Believe me, it's a whole different feeling.

## Riding Bareback

After the stationary exercises, it's time to ride. With both hands on the reins, ride to the round-pen perimeter and walk around it. Or, if you have a helper, have him take you to the fence and simply walk you around the pen. Go both ways.

Once you relax at a walk, ask for a trot and go both ways. Put one or both hands in the mane for stability if you desire. Depending on your horse's pace, the trot is the hardest gait to sit. With a quick pace or an especially bouncy horse, you might have to post the trot if it's too difficult to sit. Eventually, work up to a canter, which, because of its rocking-chair movement, should be easier to sit. Some horses are more comfortable one direction than the other. You'll discover that quickly bareback.

Using a surcingle or bareback pad is certainly acceptable. With them, you'll have more to hang on to and the pad acts as a cushion between your seat bones and your horse, especially if your horse's back is bony or has high withers.

Once you're confident in your ability to stay on your horse bareback, go from the round pen to a larger arena. It's helpful to have someone else horseback in the arena to be company for your horse. Remember his herd-animal instincts.

Safety should always be first in your mind, but when you feel good about riding bareback, venture outside the confines of the arena. Explore some trails and different avenues. Ride with only your halter and lead, then advance to just a neck rope, and finally totally bareback and bridleless. Be smart, go slow and realize that progress is a function of time and intensity. Have fun.

*Sit up and swing your right leg over your horse's rump. You'll end up sitting sideways on your horse's side. From here, reverse the procedure.*

## True Story: Bare Essentials

*Years ago, I worked as a guide, taking hunters deep into the Sierra Mountain wilderness, where motorized vehicles aren't allowed. On one particular trip, I was one of two wranglers left to care for a string of packhorses. The other guides with the saddle horses were supposed to come back the next day, so we could pack out. Unfortunately, they never showed up.*

*The only way to get the packhorses back to the station was to ride them and, as packhorses, they had no riding saddles. That meant we had to ride bareback. The trail was at least 12 miles long and, even for an experienced rider, that distance can be tough bareback. Part of the ride was done at night in pitch dark. Luckily, we made it back in good order.*

*The ride taught me just how much I had to use my legs when I ride bareback. We were in the mountains, traversing switchbacks in steep terrain, crossing rivers and climbing over downed timber. With no saddle, I had to rely strongly on my feel and balance.*

*You might not want to ride 12 miles, but riding bareback can certainly develop your riding skills.*

# 9

# GROUND WORK, THE FOUNDATION

Ground work is the basis for all horse training. When you actually begin to teach your horse to ride in earnest, he'll be ready if you've done your ground work and prepared him from the time he was a youngster. Preparation is the foundation for all success.

## Round Pen

The ideal place to begin training is in a round pen because it has no corners for a horse to stop in or escape to.

One of the best things about a round pen is that it allows the horse to use his strongest instinct to survive and that's to run. If your horse needs to run, let him do it. Mother Nature gave him four legs, big lungs and the gift of speed and tells him to run whenever he thinks there's a problem. You can allow your horse to do that in a round pen, but don't think of it simply as a place to gallop your horse until he's too tired to buck. It's been my experience that there are very few times when a horse is too tired to buck.

The training process is all about dealing with the horse's mind, which controls his body, legs and feet. His legs and feet are what he fights and flees with. If you can control the horse's mind, you can control the horse's body.

## Basic Ground Work

Start your training with basic ground work and by desensitizing your horse, which is all part of taking the fear out of the

*Ground work provides a solid basis for communication long before you step in the saddle.*

*Some horses are
bothered by a flag's
noise, flutter and feel.*

*Rub the flag all over your
horse's body until your
horse can tolerate it.*

*Desensitize your horse
with the lead rope.
Touch every part of his
body, from head to tail.*

horse. A horse isn't well broke unless you can handle every part of his body, including his face, legs and feet. I like to say that a horse needs to be gentle from the first whisker on his nose to the last hair in his tail. Some horses are a lot more touchy, sensitive or protective than others. Work with the horse and his particular circumstances. Be patient and take all the time your horse needs to desensitize him to your touch. The main reason for ground work is to relax your horse, to take the pressure off him, to desensitize him, to get him to accept a touch and follow a feel so he can give and yield to pressure.

The tools you need include a rope halter, 12-foot lead line, 25-foot soft cotton rope with a brass snap, a 50-foot lariat rope with a horse-handling honda and a flag. The latter is nothing more than a swagger stick (3 to 4 feet long) or you can use a short longe whip or buggy whip. Tie a plastic bag or white cloth or something fluttery on its end as a flag.

As I mentioned in the equipment chapter, some horses are quite bothered by a flag's noise and flutter. They don't know what it is. Introduce your horse to it slowly. Rub him with it until he accepts it all over his body. On a real skittish horse, you might have to start by wadding up a plastic sack in your hand and rubbing the horse with it until he relaxes and is comfortable with the material's noise and feel.

To start ground work, put a rope halter on your horse and attach a 12-foot lead line. Rub the horse all over with the lead line or use the coils of the 25-foot rope. Just like the flag, make sure the horse accepts the touch everywhere, from his muzzle, which is the most sensitive part of the horse, to the last hair of his tail.

If your horse is particularly sensitive, use the 25-foot rope instead of the 12-foot lead line because you have more line to work with should your horse become troubled by the touch. You're better able to stay out of harm's way with a 25-foot rope than a 12-foot one. You also can use your flag to touch him and still stay safe. *Remember:* Safety in all things comes first.

Any time your horse becomes frightened, take away the lead line, rope or flag. Never force anything on your horse. Quietly present it to him again, and if he becomes nervous, take it away again. Do this until he realizes it won't hurt him.

## Further Desensitization

After he accepts you rubbing him with the lead line, rope or flag, further desensitize his body and legs with more rope work. For this, it's best to use a 25-foot rope because of its extra length.

Start on your horse's left side. Place the rope around your horse's left front leg and run it up and down until the horse becomes used to it. When he does, hold the rope around his fetlock, with some pressure. When he yields (picks up his foot), release the pressure. Immediately give the foot back to the horse. This is his reward for yielding and it's the response you want.

Next, place the rope around the horse's heart-girth where the cinch will go. Desensitize him with gentle rubbing. Show him that it's not going to hurt. Apply pressure

### Imprint Training

People often ask me what's the best time to start a young horse, and I tell them, "The day he's born." If you have the opportunity to raise your own foal, try to be present at his birth and become a part of his life. You want him to think of you as anything else that's natural — the sky, the earth, the trees and his dam. Ideally, you want him to look upon you as part of his world. Don't turn it into a training session; it's more of an introduction to man. This at-birth process is called imprint training.

I won't go into deep detail about imprint training, but it entails touching and handling the foal in a way that takes the fear out of the horse. (For more on imprint training, see *Western Horseman's Imprint Training of the Newborn Foal*, by Robert M. Miller, DVM.) Some of the things Dr. Miller recommends are putting your fingers in the foal's ears, mouth, and nose and under his tail. These things help prepare the foal for when you tack him up with a halter, bridle or saddle or handle him when he's sick or injured. He won't be afraid of the familiar touch. The foal, as he grows older, will remember these feelings. Imprint training has an effect on him for the rest of his life. He never seems to forget it. Most horses that are imprinted correctly or handled at birth usually allow you to handle them later on. It's easier to clip, shoe, medicate or ride them if they've been handled properly in the beginning.

*Use a 25-foot rope to further desensitize your horse. Put it around your horse's left front leg and rub it up and down until your horse is accustomed to it. Then, put tension on the rope to lift the leg. The second your horse lifts his leg, release the pressure and give him back his leg.*

and release on that area repeatedly. This is what you'll do someday with the cinch, so accustom him to it now.

Slide the rope down to the horse's flank area and repeat what you did at his heart-girth. This accustoms the horse to feeling something at his flank or where the back cinch would go.

Allow the rope to fall down around his hindquarters to his back legs. Rub him there as well. Let the rope fall to the ground and move your horse so that your horse's legs walk into the loop. Then, pull the horse's nose to you slightly and when you do, the hindquarters will step away. When your horse's right rear leg steps out of the loop, catch the left rear leg with the rope, so now you have it encircled like you did the front leg. Move the rope up and down, back and forth, all the way from the flank to the fetlock.

Again, when your horse is comfortable, hold his fetlock with some pressure. When he yields by lifting his foot off the ground, release the pressure and give it back.

When you've thoroughly desensitized the left side of your horse, do the same thing with the off or right side. Always work both sides of your horse. Keep him balanced on both sides.

Work on further desensitizing your horse by throwing the rope over his head or have it land between his ears — all help him become less head-shy. You're preparing your horse for the saddle and bridle and life as a riding horse.

Periodically, throughout desensitizing, make some loud noises and quick moves around your horse. As prey animals, horses don't like either; they remind them of the actions of predators. Knowing this, do it in a way that helps your horse to become better, not worse. Don't scare the horse with these tactics, just familiarize him to the loud noises and fast movement. There's a difference between scaring the horse and desensitizing him. This exercise is done not to scare the horse, but to gentle him. This further prepares your horse for living in our world, which is full of noises and strange moving objects. This is a good way to help your horse overcome spookiness.

*Place the 25-foot rope around your horse's heart-girth and apply pressure and release, just as you'd do when you adjust your cinch.*

*Accustom your horse to the feel of the rope around his flank area. He might be bothered by this, but many saddles have back cinches so it's a good time to get him over it.*

*Slip the rope down around the horse's back leg and let the horse get used to it touching him.*

Catch the horse's left hind leg with the rope and repeat the same leg desensitization exercises you did with the front feet.

Throw the rope over your horse's head and even allow it to land between the ears. This makes the horse less head-shy and prepares him for bridling.

*Every so often make quick moves or loud noises to desensitize your horse. In time and with enough repetition, you can help your horse become more gentle and more comfortable with the world around him.*

*Put your right hand on your horse's poll and your left on the bridge of his nose. Hold. The instant your horse lowers his head, release the pressure.*

***Caution:*** In desensitizing (also known as "sacking out") a horse, never tie anything to him. I've seen some people tie tarps or garbage bags with cans to a saddle to get a horse accustomed to the noise and commotion. This could make the horse go ballistic and possibly run through a fence trying to get away from the "monster" attached to his body. Some horses never get over it and are spooky the rest of their lives. Understand where the horse is coming from. He thinks the tied-on thing is there to get him. As a prey animal, he literally fears for his life. So be aware of what you do and how you present something to your horse. Accustom him to strange things slowly and with common sense.

## Drop the Head

One important thing that'll come in handy when you introduce the bridle later on is to make sure your horse gives to pressure when you handle his head. Put your right hand on his poll and your left on the bridge of his nose and hold. There's a huge difference between holding and pulling when you handle your lead rope or your

reins, or, in this case, your hands. Learn to hold the pressure, even though your horse might push against you. Just hold. Your horse will search for an answer to the pressure and eventually he'll drop his head in response. When he does, immediately release. Pat him on the neck and reward him for the correct answer. Then start again. Hold and wait for him to drop his head. In no time at all, your horse will drop his head to the slightest pressure from your hand on his poll or nose.

## Follow a Feel

You also can teach your horse to guide from the ground, which will be helpful when you're on his back. With him facing you, throw or place the rope along the right side of his body around his hindquarters and continue on around to his left side. Hold the end of the rope steady. To escape that pressure, your horse will turn to the right 360 degrees and face you again. In doing so, he's just learned to "follow a feel," which

*This horse is "following a feel" of the rope. Initially, have the horse face you. Place the rope around the horse's side and behind his rump. With slight pressure ask the horse to follow the suggestion of the rope. The horse should turn 360 degrees and end up facing you again.*

## A BETTER WAY

### Recommendations on Early Handling

The best place for a mare and newborn foal is out on pasture if you have those facilities. It's the most natural atmosphere in which to raise a young horse. Stall-bound foals don't get nearly the mental and physical exercise they need for proper development. That's not to say that you can't have the mare and foal in a stall or corral situation part of the time, say at night or in inclement weather, but try to let the pair out to move about and graze as much as possible.

Bring them up from time to time; brush the mare and the baby, handle them both.

Halter-breaking the foal is a slow and careful process. Be patient. It's a matter of holding, not pulling, and presenting things slowly to gain the horse's confidence. Soon you'll have the horse haltered, and yielding to pressure. If he feels he needs to fight it, or sits back, that's okay. In time, he'll learn to yield to the rope. He learns that every time he gives, you'll give and soon he'll yield to the pressure on his own. This is just another way to take the fear out of the horse.

Another good early-learning experience is to have the farrier trim your horse's feet from time to time. By being handled early on, the foal is a much more solid citizen by the time he's weaned.

*For many reasons, the best place for mares to raise their foals is out on pasture.*

Try to wean your foal with another weanling. It's easier on the foal psychologically if he has a friend at weaning time and isn't alone. This removes a lot of stress from the youngster's life. Remember that you're dealing with a herd animal, and it's important that he always be part of a herd.

Plus, when he's around other horses he learns the manners of the herd. He'll learn how to handle himself around other horses so that later on, when you ride him with other horses, he knows how to behave around them.

translates to rein pressure someday. Do the same thing on the left.

If, at any time during this process, your horse becomes frightened and moves away, let him. Remember, don't force anything on the horse. You can still control him with the 25-foot rope attached to his halter.

## Forward Movement

At some point, after you've thoroughly desensitized your horse's body, it's time to ask for forward movement. It's the one thing you must have to train any horse. You can't train a horse if he won't move. It's the one thing you must insist upon.

You're still in the round pen at this point with your horse on the 25-foot line. It's easier to use the 25-foot rope (or you can use a 50-foot lariat rope) because you have better control. The rope is your line of communication and helps your horse understand what you want.

You control your horse's movement by the way you position yourself. You either drive

*Standing at your horse's hindquarters, ask for forward movement by smooching, clucking or using your flag or swagger stick on the horse's hip. Note: Craig is using a 12-foot lead rope, but a 25-foot line is best for most people.*

*After your horse has made several circles, ask him to face you by applying pressure on the rope.*

# HERE'S HOW

### Yearling Education

You can do fun things with a yearling, such as teaching him good basics on the ground, many of which are listed in this chapter. However, don't turn things into too much of a training process because a yearling is still a young horse. His attention span is short, but that doesn't mean you can't still have fun with him.

Work with him on the halter and lead rope, asking him to bend and flex his head and neck, and teaching him to yield to the rope. This can be part of the same guiding system you use when you ride on his back.

If you teach your horse good ground manners, they'll translate to the saddle someday. Horses that have good ground manners are usually the better riding horses.

In a stall, round pen or some small, enclosed area, introduce your young horse to some of the gear he'll have to wear next year, such as the saddle blanket. Rub it all over to get him used to the feel. Put it up on his neck and back, even down his hindquarters.

Continue to handle his legs and feet because that really helps at trimming and shoeing time.

Begin trailer-loading sessions at a young age. Take your horse on short trips around the block to get him used to the trailer's motion and starting and stopping.

Teach him how to longe. (See Chapter 12, "Longe-Line Techniques.") Put obstacles in the corral that he has to walk or jump over, such as small jumps, tarps, poles, etc. You can even longe your horse through water and over uneven terrain. Be creative and make it fun for your horse to learn. By exposing the young horse to different things without overexposing him, you allow him to become part of the ranch or barn activities.

Your horse will learn how to mingle not only with other horses, but also with human beings. By the time your horse is old enough to ride, he's ready. He's prepared, and that goes a long way to making a nice horse in the long run.

*Introduce a yearling to tack, such as saddle pads, early. Allow him to look at and smell it before you rub it all over his body.*

your horse into forward movement or head him off to make him stop or turn.

For forward movement, stand toward your horse's hindquarters and motion with your rope, smooch or cluck or wave your flag to ask your horse to move. You must create energy to communicate to your horse that you want him to move.

Once your horse moves forward, stop applying pressure. Allow him to travel at his chosen pace around the pen. Then ask him to stop by heading him off or taking a step toward his head or forequarters in a blocking motion and saying "whoa." The moment he does, release all pressure.

If he doesn't stop, try blocking him again and keep it up until he does. You also can cut the ring in half and block him off repeatedly. This will create a lot of direction changes or work for the horse, which will be his incentive to stop. As before, make the wrong thing work and the right thing relief.

You can ask your horse to face you, which shows an acceptance of you on his part. Do so by holding pressure on the rope until the horse turns and faces you. When he does, offer him rest, relief, relaxation and reward. Let him breathe and think about what he's just done. Go over to him, pat him on the neck and reassure him that he's done well. You want your horse to always think that being with you is the good spot, the sweet spot, the spot where he won't have to be afraid.

If your horse has been traveling to the left, ask him to go to the right by positioning yourself on his right side and asking for forward movement again. As I said before, work both sides of the horse equally.

One of the more difficult situations in which you might find yourself is having a horse who won't move or one who challenges you. You've got to be able to outthink the horse and get forward movement. There are several ways to approach this problem. One of the easiest, most effective and most natural ways is to bring in another horse, preferably a gentle, broke horse. That way you can utilize the strong herd instinct to help overcome this problem. Create forward movement with the gentle horse and the green horse will naturally follow him, thus achieving forward movement.

It's important to be able to read your horse throughout this process. Your horse will tell you how much or how little he accepts what you've been doing to him. If he stands there relaxed with his head down, a quiet look in his eye, and even licks his lips and blinks his eyes (signs of understanding and acceptance), then you know that he's grasped your message and is ready to move on.

On the other hand, if he stands there stiff with his head stuck up in the air and a wild, uncertain look in his eye, then you know he's confused and scared. (See Chapter 2, "Reading the Horse.") You'd better go back and repeat the basics until he's comfortable with what you're doing.

Ground work is good for any horse, any age and with any kind of problem. In fact, if you have a difficult horse, always go back to basic ground work first. These basics tell you where the horse is good, where he's bad, where he needs some help. Learn to listen to your horse. You can use these basics with any horse from weanlings on up to unstarted 2-year-olds, green horses and even older horses that haven't been ridden in a while. This is good for any horse, any age.

## True Story: Spoiled Rotten

A lady brought a young sorrel gelding to one of my colt-starting clinics at the Double Horn Ranch. She said the horse had been imprinted at birth, and to quote her she told me, "This horse was born into my arms." Now, this can be good or bad. Proper imprinting can make a lasting and positive impression on a horse. However, improper imprinting can be a disaster that lasts a lifetime.

In this horse's case, imprinting was a catastrophe. The horse was like a spoiled child. He did only what he wanted to do. Oh, to be sure, he had no fear of humans, but he certainly had no respect either. When spoiled to that degree, a horse often shows strong resentment when asked to do anything. This gentle, but spoiled horse had no discipline, and all creatures need discipline to learn and grow. The lady had created a monster, and this monster could buck!

I kept the gelding for several months, and, although I put a nice handle on the athletic, little horse, he was prone to out-of-control temper tantrums. Out of the clear blue, he'd sit back while standing tied and throw wild-horse fits. In the middle of a ride, for no reason, he'd come unglued. Although he'd carried packsaddles, was hobble-broke, had been ponied and even schooled in advanced leading, he never got over his spoiled attitude. His resentment of work and insistence on having his own way were nothing more than the result of improper handling from day one. Like elephants, horses never forget. I told his owner that as a green rider she shouldn't ride him. Even though he now had a good handle, he was still untrustworthy and dangerous.

Be careful of the way you handle your horse. You might think you're not teaching him something, but the horse is always learning. Make sure your horse is learning something good, whether you're on on the ground or on his back.

Oh, whatever happened to the sorrel gelding? The last I heard he was still living the spoiled life with his owner.

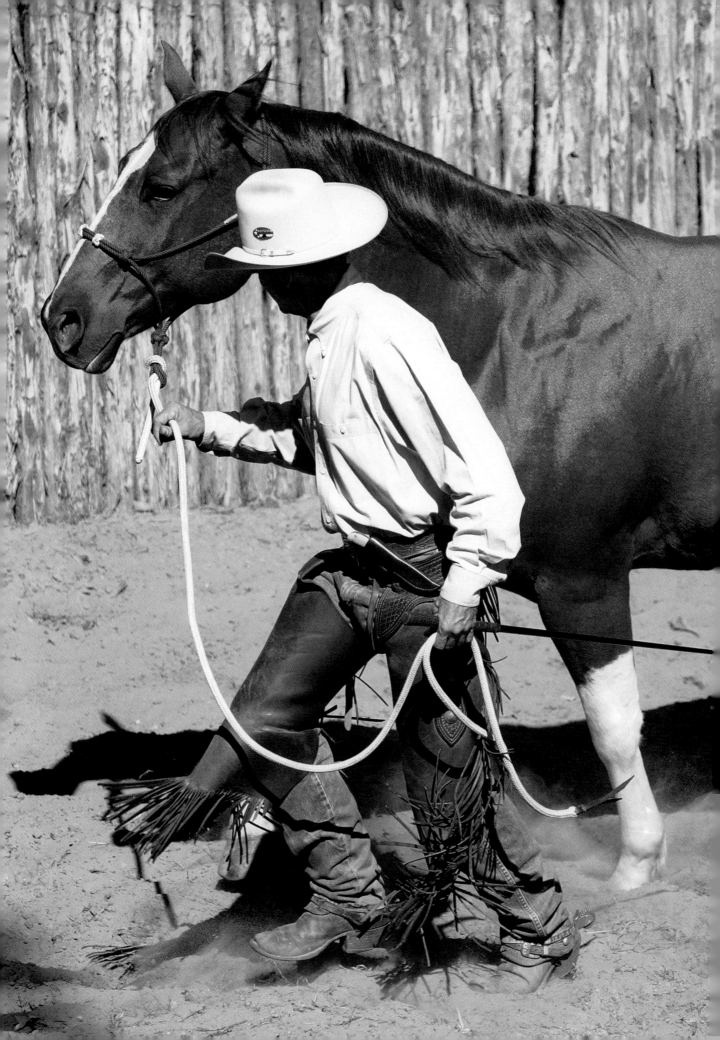

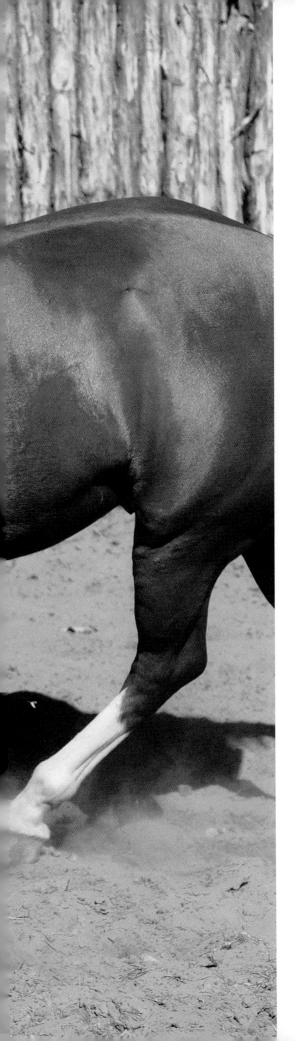

*"It's like a dance—
there's a leader and a follower."*

# 10
# LEADING AND ADVANCED LEADING

After your horse comprehends the basic ground-work lessons, he's ready for the next step: to lead properly. Leading is an extension of ground work.

Your horse should lead well in many different ways. You should not only be able to lead him from his head, as is typical with a halter and lead rope, but also lead him from a rope around his heart-girth, or on his front or hind feet. If you take the time and effort, you can even put a rope around your horse's tail and lead him backward. Actually, there are times when you'd want to lead a horse backward — unloading out of a trailer, for one.

In other words, your horse should be able to give to pressure everywhere and anywhere. The better a horse leads, the more schooled and responsive he is.

## Preparation for Leading

One way you can prepare for proper leading, which will also prepare your horse for hobbling later, is to place a 50-foot lariat rope around one of your horse's front fetlocks. Hold slight pressure on the rope and wait for your horse to step forward. When he does, immediately release the pressure as a reward.

Your horse might resist, even stomp his feet or rear. Remember, that's natural. Your horse is trying to rid himself

*Your horse should lead willingly at whatever speed you choose.*

*The second your horse takes a step forward, release your pressure on the rope.*

# A BETTER WAY

## Turn Loose and Bolt

The horse that runs off the second you undo the halter is disrespectful and shows a lack of understanding. Eventually, the horse will kick, too, making this bad habit extremely dangerous. It's something you just can't tolerate in a horse.

Every time you turn your horse loose, whether it's in a stall, corral or pasture, have him turn and face you first. When you pull off the halter, you walk away from the horse, not the other way around.

If your horse gets in a hurry, don't unbuckle the halter. Let your horse hit the end of the lead rope as he runs off. Bump him back, make him walk with you, then stand still and face you as you remove the halter.

If this doesn't work, take your horse back to the basics and put him to work circling the round pen. Go through all the steps outlined in this chapter to cue him to come to you.

You can also hobble him before you remove the halter. I believe every horse should be hobble-broke and this is one of those times when it comes in handy with problem horses. (See Chapter 11, "Hobble-Breaking.")

Also, your horse might need more time standing tied. Tie him to something stout (a post or a tree) for several hours. Every so often, go by and pet him, offer him some water. Let him realize that you're his friend. He'll look forward to you coming and when you do untie him, he won't be so anxious to leave.

of the "predatory" rope. Don't fight with him; release the rope instead. Wait on your horse; allow him to compose himself. Then, start again and let him find his way.

To help your horse understand what you want, try placing rope pressure at an angle, which will cause him to become unbalanced and move to stabilize himself.

The timing of when you apply pressure is crucial. Do so as your horse begins to lift his foot off the ground. That's when it's easiest for him to understand that you want him to move.

After your horse has mastered front-leg leading, teach him to lead backward by a hind leg, as well. Follow the same procedure as you did with the front feet. Place a lariat loop around a hind pastern. Apply pressure and take a step backward, hold and, when your horse makes an effort to move backward, release.

If you encounter a lot of resistance in getting your horse to move backward, have a

*You might encounter resistance when teaching your horse to lead backward by a hind leg. Just hold and wait for your horse to work it out.*

friend stand at your horse's head and, with the lead rope, motion your horse to move back at the same time you apply pressure on the horse's hind foot. Get him to move just one step at a time. Note: This little exercise is also great for dealing with kicking horses.

The point of all this is that your horse should lead from whatever part of his body to which you attach the lead rope. The horse that yields to pressure, no matter where it is, is a better-broke horse.

## Traditional Leading

The perfect place for your horse to lead is with his head at your shoulder and with slack in the lead line. It's personal preference, though, and you can teach your horse to lead a little farther forward or behind that point. Hold the lead rope in your right hand with the remaining rope coils in your left hand, along with your swagger stick or whip.

One mistake I see people make is trying to lead their horses by holding the lead rope where it attaches to the halter. This only encourages a horse to brace against you and become dull.

*Hold the lead rope in your right hand, with the coils and swagger stick in your left.*

**105**

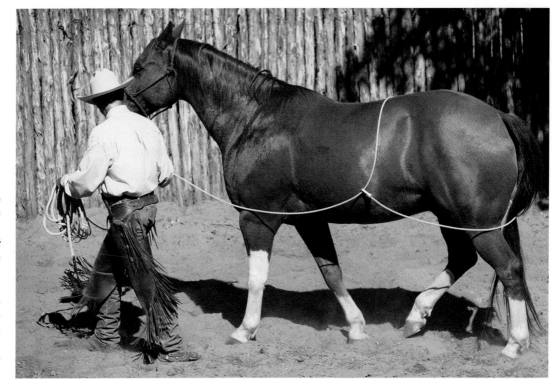

*If your horse resists the pull on the halter rope, place your lariat around his hindquarters, above his hocks. Pull when he refuses and the rope will tighten around him, thus encouraging forward movement.*

*To get your horse's hindquarters to move to the right, bend your horse's head and neck to the left with your lead rope and tap the hindquarters on the left side with your swagger stick.*

Your horse should lead on a loose line at your shoulder or whatever point you choose, but not lug on the line. Don't make the mistake of pulling harder when your horse braces against the lead rope. By nature, the horse will resist the pressure and pull back. To correct this, as you face forward leading your horse, reach behind with your swagger stick or flag and tap his rump to drive him forward.

If your horse is particularly difficult, take your 50-foot lariat rope and loop it around his hindquarters, just above his hocks. As he resists, pull on the rope. It'll tighten and drive him forward.

When you move, your horse should willingly move with you. He should walk and trot as you command. At first, simply start walking. If your horse doesn't move, reach back with your swagger stick, flag or lariat rope (if that's what you have on him) and touch him on the hindquarters. Always remember to adjust to fit each horse and each circumstance.

If you need a little more help, return to the round pen and use the wall or rails for support. Put your horse on the rail and position yourself on his left side. With your horse in the middle, ask him to move forward. Use the same system of cues as above, but now you have an immovable wall next to your horse so he has no escape route, which encourages him to move straight.

To stop, bump the lead rope with your right hand and ask your horse to "whoa." If he doesn't, put your stick in front of your horse, about chest level, and say "whoa." To get him to back, bump the lead rope, shake your stick or tap his chest and tell him to "back, back, back." Get two or three steps backward and release.

To have him trot, use a verbal command, such as a smooch or cluck, to ask for forward movement as you, too, trot out. If he doesn't, reach back with your swagger stick and tap his hindquarters. If he still resists, position a helper behind him, not too close to crowd him, and have the helper smooch or cluck to get him going.

*To stop, bump the lead rope and, if necessary, put the swagger stick in front of your horse.*

*Refine the turn cue by simply raising your hand toward your horse's face.*

**107**

# HERE'S HOW

## Tying Tips

Be careful how, where and to what you tie your horse. Always tie to something solid, such as a stout wooden post buried 3 feet and even cemented into the ground. Never tie to a gate, wire fence, portable panel or anything that can move or break.

Tie your horse fairly high, at least at his eye-level and preferably a bit higher. That way, if he pulls back, he can't get as much leverage pulling on the rope, and he's less apt to get hurt. Also, allow $1\frac{1}{2}$ to 2 feet of lead rope between the knot and the halter ring so your horse can place his head in a natural position. This gives him enough room to move around and be comfortable without getting into trouble.

Don't tie too low, short or long. A horse that's tied too low or long is apt to get his legs tangled in the rope if he paws or scratches his head on his leg. A horse that sits back when tied low can really hurt his neck.

A horse tied too short can feel trapped and panic because he feels too confined. Also, don't tie too close to another horse or yours can get kicked.

*This horse is tied to a solid metal pole, cemented into the ground.*

To get your horse to turn right on the lead rope, step toward your horse's left shoulder, put the fingertips of your right hand or the end of your stick into his shoulder blade and your left hand by his cheek and ask him to yield his shoulder to the right. This is close to a performance move on the horse's part. During this maneuver, he steps with his right front leg and crosses it with his left front leg.

Do the opposite to turn left. Step toward your horse's right shoulder and use your fingers or stick to move his shoulder to the left. In time,

you can refine this turn cue. All you'll need to do is raise your hand near your horse's head and your horse will turn his front end away.

To move your horse's hindquarters to the right, stand on the left side and bend your horse to the left with your lead rope. Touch his left rump with your stick or flag to get him to yield to the right. Do the opposite to yield to the left.

To really get your horse sharp at leading, try this little drill. First ask your horse to walk, then smooch or cluck to trot. Stop, then back. Reach back with your swagger stick and drive him forward at a walk, then trot again, walk, turn right, turn left, move his hindquarters, stop again. Mix it up until your horse pays close attention to you and your cues.

## Advanced Leading

Day by day, little by little you expand upon this; it gets better; your horse gets softer. Remember, it takes time and repetition. Soon, your horse will get so good that you can remove the halter and he'll still respond to you without a lead rope, something I call "advanced leading." He'll follow your body cues and verbal suggestions. It's like a dance — there's a leader and a follower. You walk and he walks. You trot and he trots. You back and he backs. You turn right and he goes in that direction. It can be fun and exciting for both you and your horse. It teaches your horse to be more responsive, better understand your cues and have more respect for you on the ground. Remember, the better your horse is on the ground, the better he'll be under saddle.

To begin, work in the round pen or a small corral. Take off the rope halter and 12-foot

*This horse has synchronized his movements to Craig's.*

lead line. Have your swagger stick or longe or buggy whip handy to use as an extension of your arm. Go through the above leading exercises with your horse and see if he won't follow your movements and suggestions. Because you've done this so many times, through repetition, your horse will most likely follow your lead on his own.

Where is the greatest lead rope in the world? Right between your horse's ears. Through these exercises you've developed the understanding and "want to" in your horse. He's with you because he wants to be, because it's the easy thing for him to do. You have your horse's mind and motivation. When you have both, you have perfect harmony with your horse.

If at any time, your horse leaves you, put him back to work on the rail. Make him do a few laps. Then let him find that the only resting spot is near you. Put the halter back on and get things back in order if need be, then try again.

In time, you'll have the most incredible leading horse you could ever imagine. You can move into bigger and bigger spaces and have total trust in and control of your horse. There will be an immense amount of respect between you and your horse. You can go anywhere with your horse, over jumps, through gates, into a trailer, you name it. Your horse has become a true follower and you're his leader.

*Craig's horse turns quickly to the right at Craig's suggestion.*

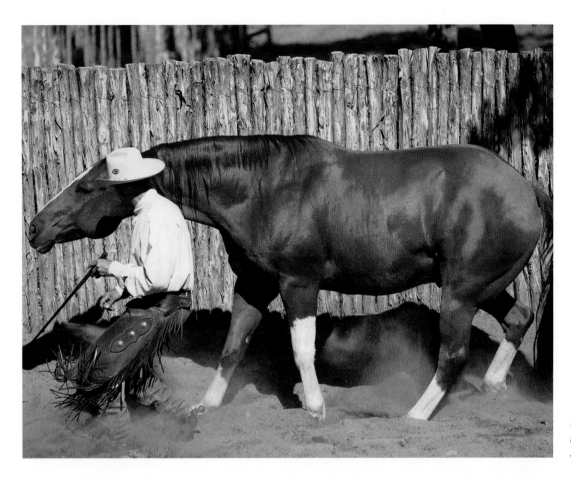

*Craig and his horse stop simultaneously.*

## True Story: Lead Well and Live

A horse who leads well can literally be a lifesaver. As a young man, I worked for several years packing horses and hunters into the rough terrain of the Sierra Mountains, near Lake Tahoe, Calif. Crossing extremely narrow mountain ledges can be harrowing, especially with a string of green riders and packhorses following behind. On several occasions, I'd have to lead nervous riders and horses over narrow ledges.

One time, our group ran into a high mountain trail that had deteriorated to the point that safety required us to get off and lead our horses across the cliff. The drop-off was on the left and we had to lead the horses on their right. One horse was so unaccustomed to the handler on his right that he spooked to the left and fell. The horse survived, but it was a lesson in the importance of quality leading.

An experienced and trustworthy horse that leads willingly and with confidence is a necessity in this situation.

A horse must lead well, follow and stand ground-tied. In tough circumstances, one bobble can be life-threatening to the rider, as well as to the horse. The secret to success is always the same — it's about basics and fundamentals. You can never do them often enough or well enough. Your life might not depend upon how well your horse leads, but again, you just never know.

**111**

*"Hobbling is one of the greatest things you can teach your horse — to give to pressure and not flee."*

# 11

# HOBBLE-
# BREAKING

Being broke to hobbles teaches a horse so many good things. He learns to stay where you put him, to have patience and to respect confinement. And someday, should the horse become tangled in wire or a hay net, it could save him from getting hurt.

## Prepare First

To teach hobble-breaking, first prepare your horse, as with anything else. Don't put a set of nylon or leather hobbles on his front legs, turn him loose and watch him struggle and possibly hurt himself. Worst of all, the first thing he learns is to run in the hobbles, which is exactly the opposite of what hobbling is all about. Accustom him to the confinement on his legs first. (See Chapter 9, "Ground Work — The Foundation," section titled "Further Desensitization" and Chapter 10, "Leading and Advanced Leading," section titled "Preparation for Leading.")

Start with a halter and 12-foot lead rope on the horse. Have a soft lariat rope with a horse-handling honda (one that releases quickly) handy. Run the lariat rope around the left front leg and rub the horse with it, up and down, until he can tolerate its feel.

Next, build a loop with the lariat and place it around the pastern of that leg. Hold the lead rope and excess coils in your left hand and work with or lead the horse with your right hand. Lead the horse in a straight line and every time he begins to pick up his left front foot, put pressure on with the lariat rope. Next, hold up the foot and stop walking. Your

*This horse will be there when his rider returns.*

*To teach your horse to hobble, accustom him to the restraint of the rope around his leg.*

*Soft, cotton Craig Cameron Training Hobbles are ideal for teaching a horse to stand hobbled.*

*Hold on to the lead rope and stay with your horse as he struggles with the hobbles. But don't stand so close as to get hurt should he jump around or rear.*

horse might fight against this, stomp and even rear. Just go with him. All horses need to be able to stand on three feet, for shoeing, trimming or doctoring. Your horse will find the easiest thing to do is give to the rope and, most importantly, that it didn't hurt him.

Desensitize all four of your horse's legs. Only when your horse is comfortable with confinement and yielding on all four legs do you tie two of them together with hobbles.

## Hobbling

I don't recommend using leather, nylon and rawhide hobbles that can possibly burn and scald when teaching a horse to hobble. I devised a set of big, wide, soft, cotton hobbles I call Craig Cameron Training Hobbles to help prepare horses during hobble-training. Once your horse is good in these, you can use any type you want.

## A BETTER WAY

### Side-line Hobbles

Fidgety horses that won't stand still for saddling, are tough to shoe, are kickers or are trailer-scramblers can benefit from being restrained with side-line hobbles. These specialized hobbles connect a front leg to its corresponding hind leg. When the horse takes a step with his front or hind hobbled leg, he finds restraint. He learns to give to pressure and to stand still in a hurry.

*Side-line hobbles connect a front leg with its corresponding hind leg and encourage a horse to stand quietly.*

**115**

Use your flag to rub the horse, then swish it all around him as if you were sacking out the horse. He should learn to put up with the pressure and stand still.

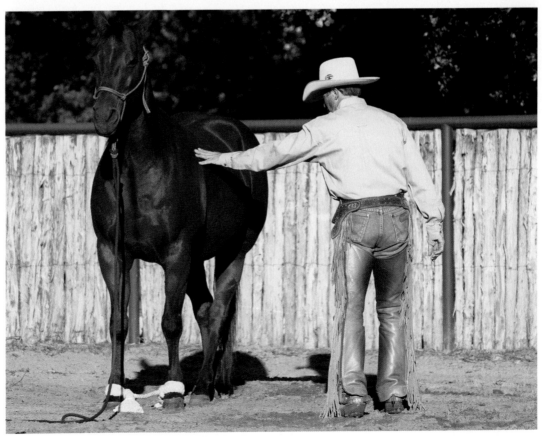

Dropping your lead rope teaches your horse to ground-tie. Walk all around him.

Put the soft, cotton hobbles on your horse's two front legs, around the pasterns. Then, don't make the mistake many people do and turn the horse loose. He can struggle, fall and hurt himself and at the same time learn to move. A hobbled horse can still move his legs. He can learn quickly to hop on his front legs, then run and really cover ground, which is what you don't want.

Hobbling is supposed to teach a horse to stand still, so don't turn your horse loose. Hold on to his lead rope while he experiments with moving his legs. He'll probably get a little nervous. He might even rear. He could stumble and fall forward, so don't stand near his front end.

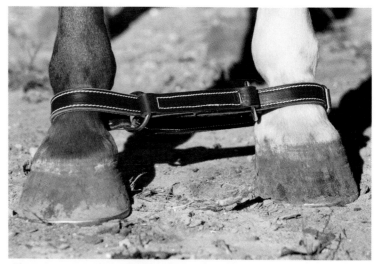

*After your horse is accustomed to soft cotton hobbles, he'll make the adjustment to regular leather hobbles just fine.*

*You can tie your reins to the hobbles or around the horse's pastern to further teach a saddled horse to stay put. This method also keeps a horse from running in the hobbles. Tie the horse's head at a comfortable level.*

**117**

Let your horse figure out that he's restrained, but that he can give to the pressure and it's okay. In the beginning, leave the hobbles on for only 10 or 15 minutes, just enough to introduce them to your horse.

After several sessions, bring out your flag and rub him with it, then swish the flag all around him. Your horse should give to the pressure and stand still. Hobbling is one of the greatest things you can teach your horse — to give to pressure and not flee. He'll know you're trustworthy and won't hurt him.

## Ground-Tie

In time, you can drop your lead rope on the ground and, in effect, you've taught your horse to ground-tie. Walk all around him, rub him, let him know it's okay for you to move around him while he's hobbled. You can now safely walk off and your horse will stay put.

There might come a time in the future when you have to ground-tie your horse, out in the pasture or on a trail, because there's no suitable place to tie him. Your horse will remain stationary when you drop the reins because he's been taught to stand still when you do so.

If you need to reinforce this, tie your reins or lead rope to the middle of the hobbles with your horse's head in a low, but natural position. Or, if you've left the halter on your horse's head underneath the bridle, which many people do when they trail ride, you can tie your lead rope to the hobbles. When your horse thinks about moving his front feet, he'll bump himself. It won't take long for him to get the hint. He'll learn that the easiest and most comfortable thing to do is stand still.

If you use mecate reins, you can also tie the lead-rope portion to a front foot and your horse will assume he's hobbled. He'll be there when you get back from whatever you're doing.

## True Story: Kicking Mare

There was a lady who wanted to come to one of my horsemanship clinics, but she didn't think she could because her mare kicked badly. She couldn't ride her horse in public. I told her to bring the horse and if I couldn't fix her, the lady wouldn't have to pay.

I put the horse in the round pen and prepared her for hobbling with the leg-yielding exercises. By the time I was done, I could get the mare to lead by any of her four feet.

I then hobble-broke her and eventually put on a set of side-line hobbles (soft, cotton hobbles that attach a front leg to its corresponding hind leg).

I rode in on my horse and circled the mare. I flagged her and she tried to kick, but the side-line hobbles prevented her from doing so. I got close to her, rubbed her and she finally realized she could tolerate me being around her.

The mare found that the herd was a good thing again. She went back to her natural instincts and worked within the herd situation. She turned loose, relaxed and stopped being dominant, aggressive and protective.

Her owner then was able to ride her in the clinic in the midst of other horses. When I looked over at the lady on her horse, I found her grinning from ear to ear.

# HERE'S HOW

There are times when you won't have a set of hobbles handy and need something to make your horse stay put. In an emergency you can make a pair out of a lead rope.

1. Take four wraps of a lead rope around your hand.

2. Slip the coiled rope off your hand and hold the four coils in that hand. There will be a hole formed by the coils.

3. Take the slack of the top coil and pull it through the hole you've made.

4. Pull enough slack through the hole to form a loop.

5. Lift the bottom coil through the hole to come out the opposite side of the hole.

6. Form a loop with it as well.

7. You should now have two loops formed at the ends of the four-coil rope.

8. Pull the loops to tighten the coils around the formed loops. Slip each loop around your horse's pasterns. To tighten, simply pull the slack on each end.

*"The better your horse is on the ground, the better he'll be when you're on his back."*

# 12
# LONGE-LINE TECHNIQUES

Your horse should be responsive whether you're on the ground or up on his back. With good longe-line techniques, you'll find that your horse relaxes and relates to you. It's a fun way to warm up your horse and it uses his energy in a constructive manner.

One of the many benefits to longe-line exercises is that you teach your horse to have trust, respect and confidence in you on the ground first. Later, that translates to the saddle.

Longeing, the way I describe it below, has nothing to do with tiring the horse out so he doesn't have as much energy when you ride him. It has to do with getting control of the horse's mind. If you have that, you have control over his body.

## In the Beginning

The best place for longe-line work is in a round pen. Its small diameter is perfect and provides a rail to guide your horse around. Later, you can progress to outside the pen, but for now, begin your lessons in a small space.

Put a halter with a 12-foot lead rope on your horse. A 12-foot rope gives you plenty of room to work without being too short or too long in the beginning. As you progress, you can move up to your 25-foot and even 50-foot ropes. Also, have a longe whip handy to use as an extension of your arm.

Longe-line work is just like reined work. You're trying to control the whole horse — head, neck, shoulders, rib cage

*A round pen is the best place for longeing lessons. Put a halter and 12-foot lead rope on your horse for control. Later, you can graduate to longer-length ropes or outside the pen.*

**121**

and hindquarters — and all facets of the horse's movement — right, left, up, down, back and forth.

The following exercises can be fun and refreshing for both you and your horse.

## Work on the Longe-Line

As in most other exercises, controlled forward movement is the essential ingredient with your horse. To encourage forward movement, move or shake your longe whip at your horse. You can also use the tail end of your lead rope in a circular motion. Create this energy in your rope to stimulate your horse's forward-movement response.

The mistake I see a lot of people make is that they literally chase a horse's hindquarters in an effort to get him to move. It looks like the horse is longeing them. The first movement is simply a circle around you, but you shouldn't be the one doing all the moving.

Say you want to circle your horse to your right. First you must prepare and position yourself and your horse. Hold the lead rope in your right hand and the longe whip in your left. If your horse is already facing sideways to the right, shake your whip or tap him on the right hindquarters, suggesting he move forward. In this case, your right hand is your sending hand and your left hand is your driving hand.

If your horse is facing you instead of standing sideways, use your longe whip to

*To get your horse to move to your left, hold the lead rope in your left hand and shake the tail end of the lead rope or your longe whip at your horse's left shoulder.*

*Ask your horse to move around you on a loose line.*

ask his shoulders to move in the direction you want him to go. In other words, if you want your horse to move to the right, shake the longe whip at his right shoulder or tap him there asking him to move right. Your right hand is outstretched in a sending fashion and your left hand drives the hindquarters. When he yields away from you, he'll face the desired direction of travel. Then, use your whip or lead-rope tail to drive his hindquarters into a forward-movement circle.

As your horse moves around you, you might have to move with him because of the short length of your 12-foot lead rope. (If 12 feet seems to short, move up to your 25-foot line.) With the 12-foot line, you're most likely working at a walk or trot. You don't have a lot of room for cantering. Later, as your horse progresses to a longer longe line, you can remain stationary in the middle of the pen, pass the line behind you and your horse will do all the work, at all gaits. But right now you might have to move with him at his hip to encourage forward movement. Remember, you're either driving your

horse or you're heading him and, in this case, you want to drive your horse forward by staying at his hip.

## Change Directions

To change directions, prepare ahead of time. Change your lead rope and longe whip hands. In other words, if you're longeing to the right and want to change directions to the left, put your lead rope in your left hand and your longe whip in your right.

Here, understanding the mechanics of the horse helps you get a direction change. Don't try to change directions until you've disengaged your horse's hindquarters. Just like in one-rein work, bend your horse toward you by shortening your rope. That disengages his hindquarters to the outside of the circle and he'll face you. When he does, send your horse to the left by bumping him on the left shoulder with the longe whip or tail of your lead rope. When he turns in that direction, drive his hindquarters by bumping his left hip with the whip.

*When you change directions, change hands. Put your lead rope and longe whip in the opposite hands.*

The changing-directions maneuver, if done correctly, teaches your horse to work off his hindquarters.

## Longeing in Motion

Once your horse gets into the longeing mode, don't continually drive him with your whip. That makes him dull to your cues. Use it only if he slows down; then use it to drive him. See how little it takes to get the job done.

Your objective is to work on a loose line. All your horse's movements should happen when there's slack in the line. When you have that going for you, your horse is longeing correctly and tuned in to you. It's all about lightness in your horse's responses. Your horse is always looking for the release — either on the ground or in the saddle. If you pull on your horse, he'll pull back. He'll stiffen and brace against you. That's not longeing; that's a battle of wills and a tug of war you might lose.

*To get your horse to back up, have him face you in the middle of the pen, so there's room behind him. Bump the lead rope or shake it vigorously creating energy until your horse takes one step back, then release your pressure. Build upon that.*

*Reel your horse in and let being near you be the resting spot.*

## Back-and-Forth Exercise

This is an excellent time to teach your horse to back and this exercise will help you do that. Stand in the middle of the pen, in front of your horse, leaving him room behind to move back. Try any of the following to get a backward response: Gently bump the lead shank and say "Back." Or press your fingertips or longe whip on your horse's chest. Also, try shaking your lead rope vigorously, sending lots of energy down the line. Recognize that your horse won't know what you want and he'll have to figure it out. Build off his first step or slightest try to move backward. Stop bumping or shaking when he does. The second he stops moving backward, shake or bump again. He'll take a few more steps back. Stop when he does. In time, it'll take very little for him to march backward at a good, deliberate clip on a loose rein.

To bring the horse to you, smooch or reel him in with the rope. You might even walk backward a step or two yourself. That encourages a horse to come forward. Let him find a resting spot in front of you. Rub him and let him think that where you're at is where he's safe and doesn't have to work hard.

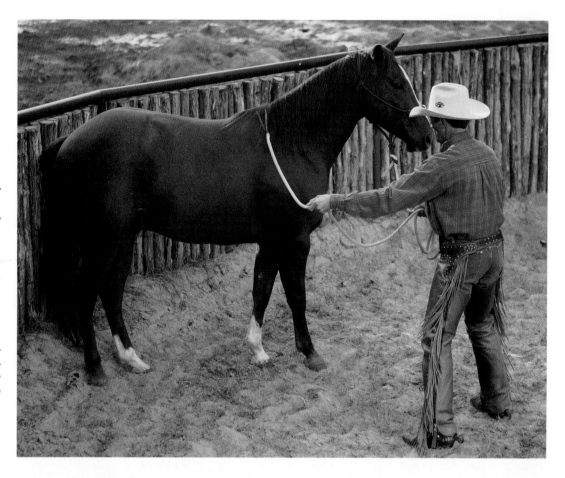

*To teach your horse to move laterally or side-pass, have him face the middle of the pen, with his hindquarters on the rail. Stand to one side of the horse, block his forward movement with your halter and lead rope and swing the tail end of the rope at his shoulder until he takes one step sideways.*

## Lateral-Movement Exercise

You can teach your horse to move laterally or side-pass in the round pen. Put his hindquarters on the rail with his nose facing toward the center of the pen. To move to the right, stand on his left side. Now, everything is open to your horse's right and closed or blocked behind him and to his left. Swing the tail end of your lead rope first at your horse's left shoulder, then at his left hip. If necessary, tap him with it lightly. You're asking your horse to yield to pressure. It's a smooth, methodical movement that should cause him to move his front end and hindquarters sideways. As soon as he moves sideways even the slightest, stop swinging as a release. Block any forward movement with your lead rope and walk next to your horse as he moves down the rail.

To side-pass left, stand on your horse's right side. Block forward movement with your halter and lead rope as you swing your lead rope's tail end at your horse's right shoulder and hip.

## A BETTER WAY

### Longe-line Safety

The safest and easiest way to handle your longe line and longe whip is to keep your equipment organized. Coil the longe line in a way that it's easy to feed out by simply opening your hand. Practice coiling your longe line the same way a cowboy coils his lariat rope.

Also, become proficient in using the longe line in either hand. If your horse is traveling to the right, your longe line should be in your right hand and the longe whip in your left. Do the opposite to the left.

Safety dictates never putting your arm through the coils of the longe line, where it can become tangled, endangering both you and your horse.

# Obstacles

Introducing obstacles during longe-line work is fun and it further progresses your horse. It helps him become brave, and a more courageous horse is always safer to ride.

Use all the same cues for forward, backward and sideways movements that you did in the longeing lessons, only now you're adding another element.

For example, you can place a rolled-up plastic tarp in the round pen and ask your horse to step over it. You're not only incorporating forward movement, you're also asking your horse to cross or work an obstacle. As he becomes comfortable with stepping over it, you can open it bigger and bigger until he walks over it, stands on it, backs over it or even moves sideways across it.

*Place a folded tarp perpendicular to the rail and let your horse check it out if he feels the need.*

*In time, your horse will be comfortable with walking, then trotting and cantering over it.*

**127**

*Small jumps are
fun obstacles for
your horse. Also,
they can teach him
to become more
brave, plus more
trusting in you.*

# HERE'S HOW

### Longe-line Jumping

A good obstacle to use in longeing is a set of two or three
barrels. (I use plastic 50-gallon drums.) Lay them on their
sides perpendicular and up against the rail or wall of a
round pen. Ask your horse to longe over them, first at a trot
and then a lope. Allow him to go past them a time or two
and then longe him up to them. It's okay for him to stop and
check them out. While they might seem intimidating to him
at first, in time, he'll find them easy to jump.

It's a little more challenging than low poles, but the barrels
create confidence and courage. This exercise creates better
balanced and more coordinated horses.

Horses seem to have fun and enjoy this free-moving
longe-line technique.

*Allow your horse to
inspect the barrels
before you ask him to
longe over them.*

*A confident horse will
jump the barrels in style.*

Try placing a small jump in the pen, simple cross poles, only a foot or so high, or an easy water crossing. Ask your horse to trot over it. Now you're getting not only right, left, back and forth, but also up and down.

What you don't want to do is force your horse over a scary obstacle. If he needs to go around it, let him. Never fight with your horse while he's trying to learn. If he needs to stop, look at and smell it, let him. He might even paw at it. Any time his head is down and he's smelling or pawing at an obstacle, he's thinking about it. Give him the time he needs.

You'll find your horse learning to learn. He'll enjoy the interaction and the challenges. They're things he can do, and he has fun doing them for you. His confidence will grow, not only in himself, but in you.

In time, you can move from using the 12-foot lead rope to a longer longe line and from the round pen to an arena. The added distance or extra space shouldn't bother your horse. He'll be able to make the transfer easily. Then, venture outside the confines of rails and longe in the open. Find natural obstacles to work and watch your horse advance by leaps and bounds.

Working on the longe line is like anything else. Don't try to get it all done the first day. Take a few steps at a time. Remember not to get upset, angry or impatient. All that will do is get in your way. Recognize that your horse is only doing what he thinks he's supposed to do. By being patient and consistent in your training, you'll give your horse a better chance at comprehension. Present it to him in a way he can understand and then give him the time it takes to understand. Do that and you can accomplish an amazing amount in an amazingly short time.

## True Story: Silly Filly

*I built my reputation on troubled and problem horses that have been started incorrectly or have had bad experiences with human beings. To get through to these frightened animals, I had to find a way to regain their confidence.*

*A typical example is a young mare that had been traumatized on her first saddling. The saddle had gotten underneath her and scared her to death. She was brought to me for help. All her confidence was gone; she wouldn't even lead or stand tied. She'd panic, sit back and literally almost kill herself by beating her head and body against whatever she was tied to. This mare had real problems. I called her "Silly Filly."*

*To help her, I went back to square one and did the normal round-pen and gentling process. However, the real* *confidence and trust I believe was re-established with longe-line work. This frightened mare took some time, but with patience I made progress by longeing her over my obstacle course, which contains jumps, tarps, barrels, ups and downs and even water crossings. Although challenging to the horse, it gives them someplace to go and something to do.*

*Silly Filly began to enjoy this process. In time, she was doing the course while carrying the saddle. I ponied her from another horse and eventually I began to ride her without problems. The longe-line course was the perfect solution. I accomplished what I needed to do without pain or fear. Horses seem to love this type of work. It becomes fun for them, and I think they look forward to it. Advanced longe-line work makes for brave horses. Before Silly Filly went home I began calling her by her real name, Pretty.*

# 13

# PREPARATION FOR THE FIRST RIDE

There isn't really a set pattern to starting a young horse, because every horse is an individual, and you need to work each horse with that in mind. Some are sensitive, others are lethargic and each can be challenging. As a horseman, you should fit the horse, the situation and the circumstance, and those can change on a moment-to-moment, day-to-day basis.

In this chapter, I'll give you some general guidelines — things that work well for me.

## Introduce the Pad

First, introduce your tack and gear to your horse in the confines of a round pen or small corral with your horse outfitted in a halter and lead rope. From the beginning, don't hide anything from him. Start by offering your saddle pad. Let him look at and smell it. Present it to him and rub him all over with it. Move it all the way up to his neck and ears and then back to his hindquarters, down to his hocks. Work both sides. When he's unperturbed, casually fling it over his back, back and forth until he's at ease with the movement in both of his eyes. Remember that horses don't see as we do. When you're working on your horse's left side, the horse sees you mostly with his left eye and the same goes for the right side. When he's relaxed with this activity (and this could take several minutes to much

*Driving helps prepare a horse for his first ride.*
*He experiences the feel of being guided by reins.*

longer for sensitive horses), lay the pad on his back and let him feel it.

If your horse is a little nervous and moves around instead of standing still, that's okay. Put him to work by moving the hindquarters, or, in other words, making the wrong thing work and the right thing easy. Send him around the pen a time or two, then offer him a chance to stand again. Throw the pad up over his back and rub him with it until he stands still.

*Allow the horse to see and smell the pad.*

## Introduce the Saddle

When he stands quietly with the pad, you're ready to introduce the saddle. (Note: When saddling your horse for the first time, never tie him to something solid. If he spooks and pulls back, he'll feel captured, then panic, possibly hurting himself. Also, this situation could create the bad habit of sitting or pulling back.) In the round pen, simply lay the rope over the crook of your left arm as you introduce the saddle. Make sure your cinches are tied up the way they should be in the keepers so they don't flail around as you swing the saddle smoothly onto your horse's back. (See "Here's How" titled "Organize Your Latigo Strap and Cinches.") If your horse moves a little bit because of his uncertainty, control him with the rope and wait for him to stand still.

This is where it really pays off to have desensitized both sides of your horse. Walk around to the right side and let the cinches down. Make sure the saddle fits your horse. I've always said there's not much riding on it except your life, so make sure your equipment fits your horse and is in good condition.

To cinch your horse, run the latigo or tie strap through the cinch ring one time and

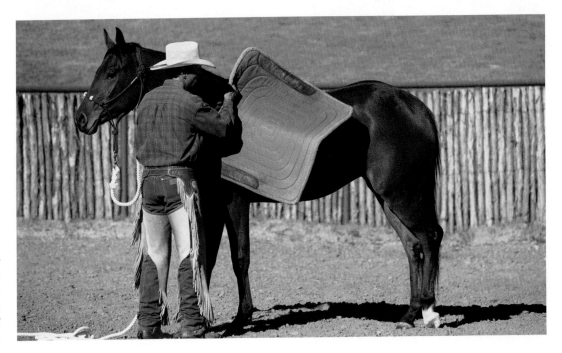

*Flip the pad over each side of the horse's back so the horse sees the movement out of both eyes.*

*Place the saddle lightly on the horse's back in one smooth move.*

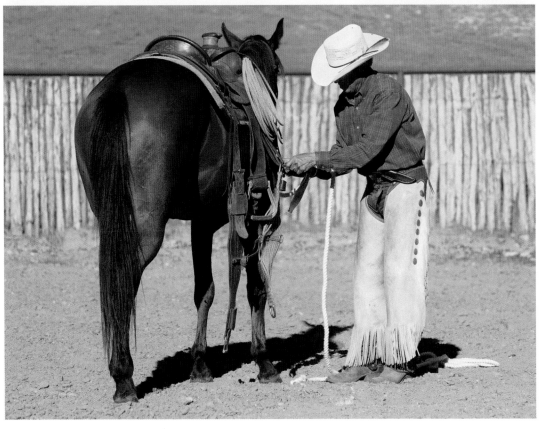

*Move to the horse's right side and take down your cinches, which should be organized and hung properly in the keepers.*

*Cinch slowly and snugly, but not too tight.*

*Take as many wraps of the latigo as you need to stabilize the saddle and put the excess latigo in the front keeper.*

*Buckle the rear cinch snugly enough so the horse can feel and accept it, but not too tight.*

pick it up slowly. Always cinch a horse gently, never with hard and fast movements. (See "A Better Way" titled "Saddle and Cinch Know-How.") Put your left hand on your horse's shoulder to stabilize him as you slowly pull the latigo with your right hand. After you pull the latigo, stop and wait for your horse to get used to the pressure. Then pull a bit more until you can snug the cinch on the horse and he accepts it. Loop the latigo around as many times as you can, so that if the horse gets loose, the saddle will stay put.

Next, adjust the rear or back cinch if your saddle is equipped with one. Any time you reach for a back cinch, keep your head in a forward position, not in the horse's flank area. You don't want to get kicked.

Just as with the front cinch, tighten the rear cinch slowly. You don't want it too tight or too loose. Its main function is to help stabilize the saddle and keep the back of the saddle from moving up and down and side to side. It also helps prevent the saddle's cantle from tilting forward on the horse during hard stops (such as in reining, cutting, roping or working cattle) or during steep descents on the trail. Buckle the rear cinch up against the horse's belly, neither too tight nor too loose, but to where he can feel and accept it.

## Stand by Your Horse

Once you've cinched your horse, don't be in a hurry to move him. A sudden start could precipitate a bucking spree as the horse feels the weight and pressure of the saddle for the first time. Instead, show your horse that he doesn't need to be afraid. Let him stand next to you, relaxed, with the saddle on his back. Then, carefully, lead him off a few steps, so he can feel the saddle's weight.

If your horse bucks, step quickly out of the way and let him buck. Allow him to work it out for himself without you being close by. You want him to figure out that the saddle, just like you, won't hurt him. When he stops bucking, walk over, pet him and reassure him. Walk him around some more until he's thoroughly comfortable with carrying the saddle.

*After you've saddled the horse, stand by him for a few minutes and let him soak in the strange feeling. Pet and reassure him.*

*Once he seems comfortable with the saddle, lead him off and let him carry the saddle.*

*Despite even the most careful preparation, some horses still buck. Stand out of the way and let the horse get it out of his system.*

## True Story: Time Bomb

*I witnessed a man who's supposed to be an experienced horseman starting a colt. He did some good things, but I think he got in a hurry. He bypassed some important steps and the horse's actions confirmed it. The horse seemed nervous and extremely protective. I think the trainer was paying more attention to the people watching than he was to the unstarted colt. The colt gave all the classic signals that he needed more work and more time. The horse looked tight and hard. He was statuesque and definitely on guard. Instead of working through understanding, this youngster was working through instinct.*

*To my unbelieving eyes, the "trainer" mounted this ticking time bomb. Before he got well-seated, the bomb exploded. After a short effort, the cowboy was on the ground.*

*This is a typical mistake that could be easily avoided. By listening to and reading the horse and taking time to take the proper steps, anyone starting a colt can have positive results.*

## Saddle Desensitization

When he's calm and quiet, ask for forward movement around the pen. Have him carry the saddle until he's totally relaxed with it. Look for the same signs of relaxation you did before — lowered head and neck, quiet or blinking eyes, licking lips.

Depending on the horse, put either the 25-foot or the 50-foot lariat rope on the horse. Ask your horse to stop and come to you with a "whoa" and a gentle tug on the rope. Draw him to you and do a few more things to acquaint him with the tack on his back. For example, with him standing next to you, "pop" the stirrup leathers by grabbing the leathers and tugging on the stirrups, flapping them against his sides. If it spooks him, stop, let him relax, then repeat until he accepts the commotion and noise. Move the saddle on his back by grabbing the horn and rocking it back and forth. Reach down and pick up the back cinch. Make sure he accepts everything about the saddle.

Next, do all these things as you pull the horse to you with the rope. Stand close by the horse's shoulder and pull his nose toward you. He'll walk toward you and circle around you. Flap the stirrups, pick up the back cinch, move the saddle horn, desensitize him to the saddle. Then, do the right side.

At this point, send the green horse off around the round pen again to see if he wants to buck anymore. Work with your horse, but don't exhaust him.

If your horse is still very sensitive or nervous, here's an exercise that'll help him overcome that.

With your 25-foot rope attached to the horse's rope halter, loop the line around one of the solid posts or struts of your round pen. Don't tie the horse hard and fast, simply place the rope around the post and snug up the horse somewhat close so you can handle him. (This is similar to the exercise to help cure the pull-back horse as described in "A Better Way" sidebar in Chapter 5.)

From here, make noises to spook the horse a little bit. Start quietly with a "shwisshh" to startle the horse, but don't scare him to death. You're asking him to face his fears. Let him figure out that you're not going to hurt him.

When the horse startles, he'll probably move backward, but he's got 25 feet of rope to do so. Let the rope out and go with him, but then pull him back in with it.

With him standing next to the fence, continue desensitization by swinging the rope around him, touching his legs with the rope (which also helps cure kicking horses), popping the stirrup leathers, rocking the saddle, etc. Do all these things until he stops spooking.

After you've worked one side thoroughly and your horse accepts the commotion, walk around the horse. He'll switch eyes, which means he'll see you with the other eye and also the other half of his brain. Go through the same procedure as above. Soon, your horse will relax all over. He'll stop jumping around and stand still, head down, licking his lips in understanding and acceptance. Just like in your earlier sacking-out exercises, you've taken the fear out of your horse.

In starting any horse, you want to desensitize him to loud noises, fast movements and any tack or gear that you might use. Later on in training you'll sensitize him to certain things (such as leg and rein cues), but right now you want him thoroughly comfortable with your touch and your equipment.

*Further desensitize the horse to the saddle by rocking the saddle horn back and forth to familiarize him with the saddle's weight and feel.*

*Pick up the stirrups and back cinch and flop them on the horse's sides. Do both sides of the horse.*

Stand at the horse's shoulder and ask him to move around you. As he does, repeat the desensitization exercises.

Release more of the line and ask the horse to move out around you.

Be prepared that he might break in two again. Let him work it out.

From time to time during the gentling process, make sudden movements, loud swishing noises, etc., to further accustom your horse to the sights and sounds he'll need to tolerate. If he can't accept them when you're on the ground, he won't when you're in the saddle either.

# Ground Driving

By now, your horse should be ready for ground driving, which is a process that prepares him for riding and being guided with reins. You'll teach your horse to turn right, left, stop and back using a set of driving lines or ropes. He learns to accept the ropes and follow a feel all at the same time. Ground driving really advances your horse, both mentally and physically.

*Attach the driving lines to the halter cheekpieces, then run them through the stirrups. Ask the horse to move forward by clucking, smooching or tapping him lightly on his haunches or hocks.*

*Wave or shake the driving lines and that will cause the stirrups to flop around. This further accustoms the horse to the feel of a rider's legs.*

*Ask the horse to back by rocking each line alternately. Release pressure when the horse steps backward. Be happy with one step at a time.*

*Work the green horse from a steady mount, if you have one. Do all the same things you did on the ground — rock the saddle horn, flap the stirrups, touch his sides, make sudden movements and loud noises. All prepare him for life as a riding horse.*

Start by snapping on two 25-foot cotton driving lines to the cheekpieces of your horse's halter and then run them through the stirrups. The setup makes it easier for your horse to follow a feel right and left.

With a line on either side of your horse, stand at a safe distance behind him and send him forward using light taps with the ropes on his haunches or hocks and/or a clucking or smooching sound. If he still won't move, put both lines in one hand and use your flag in the other hand. You have to create energy by shaking or waving your flag so your horse understands that you want forward movement.

Be careful not to get too close to your horse, though, should he decide to kick at the unfamiliar feel of both ropes. But don't stand so far away that you aren't effective either. Horses that kick usually do so out of self-preservation, not meanness. Just be careful of where you place yourself.

Drive your horse around the pen a time or two to get him used to forward movement with both lines. You also can use your lines to lift the stirrups and flop them on both sides. This further prepares your horse for the feel of the rider's legs against his sides. Then ask him to turn and change directions.

Here's how: If your horse has been moving to the left around the pen, simultaneously shorten the right line as you step toward the horse's forequarters or head. That blocks his forward movement. Add pressure with the right rein, which encourages him to bend to the right following the feel of the rope as he changes directions. This is an extension of the earlier exercise (during desensitization) in which you threw your rope around your horse and asked him to bend his body and turn.

As soon as your horse turns into the fence away from you, release pressure on the right rope and drive him out with light taps from the left rope or clucking or smooching sounds.

You should be in the correct position to drive from behind because you've already stepped to the head to stop your horse before turning. Now that he's turned, you'll automatically be at his hindquarters to drive him. But if you find you're not, take a step backward to place yourself at your horse's hips. If you're standing at his head when he makes the turn, you'll block his forward motion, which isn't what you want.

Now, ask for a stop. Hold pressure with one or both lines and say "whoa." As soon as he stops, release your hold.

To teach backing with the driving lines, create even pressure with the lines. Hold and with a slight rocking motion, wait for the right response, which would be even one step backward. Be happy with that. Release. From there, work with the horse to achieve two steps, three steps and more. Build on that and, in time, the horse will learn how to place his feet backward. Remember, it's not the pressure the horse is interested in, it's the release.

## Working from Another Horse

A lot of desensitizing work can be done from the back of another horse. I especially like to work problem horses or head-shy horses this way. It's also good for horses who haven't been ridden in a while or those who've never been ridden. Having another horse in the pen with him relaxes a green horse because he feels part of a herd and that's one of his most secure feelings. Remember, horses find safety in numbers.

However, I realize not everyone has a second horse or one that's solid enough to handle the task. This is simply an extra step

# A BETTER WAY

### Saddle and Cinch Know-How

When saddling, the best way to hold your saddle is to place it on your right hip with your right hand holding the cantle. That leaves your left hand free to handle your horse with the lead rope and adjust the saddle pad as well. Drape the lead rope in the crook of your left arm, so you can control the horse as needed. Then, with your left hand on the saddle's left front skirt, swing the saddle onto your horse's back softly, but just like you would any horse.

Don't cinch your horse so tightly that it cuts him in two, and, by the same token, don't cinch so loosely that it doesn't stabilize the saddle. That's dangerous. I've seen riders who thought they were being kind by not cinching tightly enough. A too-loose cinch can rub a gall sore as easily as a too-tight cinch.

Cinch your horse slowly, in stages. Cinch relatively loosely at first; don't just tighten the latigo in one motion. Snug the cinch a little at a time. Your horse will appreciate the consideration. This also helps prevent your horse from becoming "cinchy" or grouchy at the act of being cinched. Most horses object to quick tightening or jerking around their girths, which also can create the dangerous habit of sitting back.

So cinch slowly; tighten a little bit at a time. Walk your horse out a step or two, then tighten some more. After you've done this two or three times, you should be ready to go. A properly tightened cinch doesn't press into the horse's skin, neither does it dangle. It lies flat against the horse's side. You should be able to put your fingers under the cinch. Snug, but not tight, would be a good description for normal riding.

If you're riding for any length of time and stop to rest, give your horse a breather by loosening your cinches. It's also nice to lift your saddle off your horse's back and

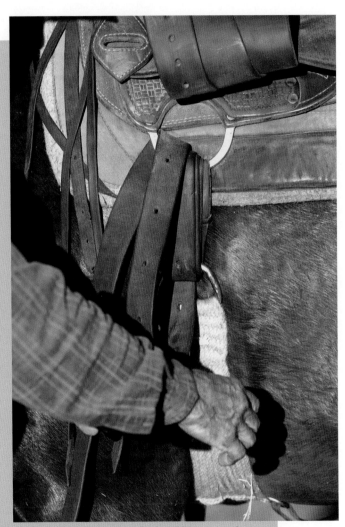

*A properly adjusted cinch should be snug, but not tight. You should be able to put your fingers under the cinch.*

let air circulate. Treat your horse the way you'd like to be treated. If it's hot out, don't tie him in the sun. Find a shady spot, loosen his cinches and let him relax.

Realize that the way you ride your horse today constitutes the kind of horse you'll ride tomorrow.

# HERE'S HOW

## Organize Your Latigo Strap and Cinches:

### Organize the Latigo

Never take the saddle off your horse without tying up the latigo strap and cinches. When you don't tie them, they drag on the ground where you or your horse might step on and/or become entangled in them. Besides that, they get dirty, which can cause cinch sores. When you care for your equipment, it'll take care of you.

1. Hold the latigo strap with your left hand about 10 to 12 inches down from the front rigging dee.

2. Grasp the remaining latigo strap with your right hand. Run it behind (or under) the strap in your left hand and up through the dee. This forms one loop held in your left hand.

3. Bring the latigo strap that you pushed through the dee ring to meet the first formed loop held in your left hand. You now have two formed loops of equal lengths, held in your left hand.

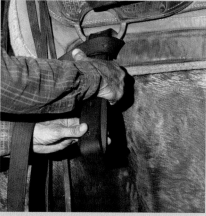

4. Take the tail end or remaining latigo slack and wrap it around the two lengths of strap.

5. Push the tail end up through the dee ring.

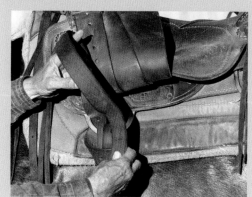

6. Pull the tail end through the loop created when you wrapped the latigo around the two formed loops.

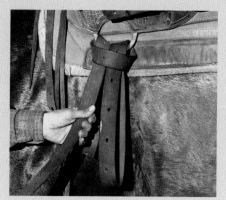

7. Tug the tail end until it's taut.

Now your saddle is ready to be carried or stored. To saddle, untie the looped portion. Pull the strap straight down, which quickly and easily releases the entire latigo strap.

# HERE'S HOW

## Organize the Off-Side Cinches

**Never twist your main cinch, which could cause a hard or uneven spot in the cinch's fibers or material. This could create a sore on your horse.**

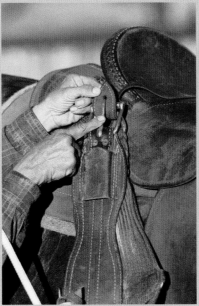

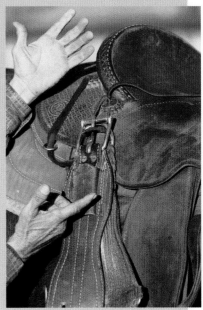

*1. Pick up the main cinch without twisting it. Then pick up the back cinch, twist it a half turn so that it rests on top of the front cinch with the buckle facing out.*

*2. With the buckle of the back cinch in front of the buckle of the main cinch insert the off-side keeper through both cinches. Use the back cinch's tongue to fasten the cinches to the keeper.*

*3. The back cinch's tongue holds both cinches neatly in place.*

you can take in preparing your horse for riding. If you don't have a horse to work from, don't worry. It's certainly not a prerequisite. However, what you can do is step up on a fence and allow your horse to see you above him. That further prepares him for mounting. Also, while on the fence, use a swagger stick and touch him all over with it. The more you handle your horse, the more ready for riding he becomes.

But if you do have a steady mount, pony (hold by the lead line) the young horse from the older horse's back. Do a lot of the same things you did on the ground to desensitize your horse — grab the saddle horn and rock it back and forth, flap the stirrup leathers, pick up on the back cinch, tip the horse's nose toward you in preparation for guiding.

With the advantage of being horseback, you also can touch the young horse's sides with your legs, accustoming the horse to that feel. Lean over his back. The young horse now has the opportunity to see someone above him for the first time, further preparing him for being ridden. It reduces the risk factor for you, as well.

When you step off the older horse and prepare to mount the young one, you can leave the older horse in the pen with you. Take off his bridle and turn him loose, but make sure he's trustworthy and not a kicker. Having another horse in the pen has a calming effect on the green horse. He's not alone. He'll be more apt to follow the older horse around the pen, and that'll help you with forward movement on your young horse.

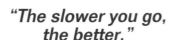

*"The slower you go, the better."*

# 14

# THE FIRST RIDE

After you've gone through all the ground work and desensitization, don't feel you have to mount and ride your young horse right away. In fact, the more ground work you can do over time, the better your horse will be prepared and the safer you'll be. Don't be in a rush; you don't have to get on him the first day.

A year later, it won't matter which day, week or month you got on your horse. Your preparation is the key. Actually the slower you go, the better. You'll know when he's ready. He'll show you the signs — he won't be nervous or skittish; he'll give to pressure; he'll "turn loose." In other words, he'll be relaxed and attentive to you. He won't be afraid, but realize his fear can come back in an instant if he misunderstands something.

## Prepare to Mount

When you've decided your horse is ready to be mounted, there are things you can do to prepare him even more.

First, pay attention to how your horse is standing. If his feet are too close together or he's got one cocked, he'll become unbalanced when you put weight on him to mount. Rock the saddle horn back and forth. That causes your horse to stand up square, with all four legs underneath him. He's less apt to move if he's standing solidly on all four legs. Then he's ready for your weight.

To mount from the left, step in the left stirrup with just the toe of your left boot. Never stick your entire boot in the stirrup

*When you get on for the first time isn't as important as how well you've prepared your horse for the experience.*

**145**

*Just before you mount, rock the saddle horn back and forth one more time to make sure your horse has his legs under him squarely.*

*With the lead rope in your left hand and your right hand holding the right saddle swell, step the toe of your left boot in your left stirrup. Don't mount, however, if your horse starts to move as the one in the photo is doing. Wait until all four feet are under the horse.*

*Step up in the stirrup, but don't mount yet. Stay balanced over your horse, who might find the need to shift his weight to accommodate you, as this youngster is doing. That's okay. Lean over the saddle, pat the right side of your horse's neck and let your horse see you in his right eye.*

*Repeat the mounting preparation on the horse's right side.*

on a green horse because if he buggered, you could hang up and be dragged.

Slowly put weight in the stirrup; grab the right saddle swell with your right hand for support and put your left hand in the mane. Step up, but don't swing your leg over yet. Stand on the side of your horse for a few moments, allowing the horse to feel your weight and get a good look at you with his left eye.

Keep your 12-foot lead rope in your left hand. Reach over your horse's neck with your right hand and rub your horse reassuringly. Now he can see you with his right eye, as well. Then, reach back and rub his hindquarters just behind the saddle, brushing the top of them, just as your leg will do.

After that, rub your horse's shoulder with your right hand, then reach down and pick up your right stirrup leather and touch the horse's right shoulder with it.

Step down and do the same thing from the right side. Accustom your horse to being mounted from both sides. This time, however, hold your lead rope in your right hand and use your left hand to desensitize your horse's left side, just as you did the right.

Frankly, we don't do enough work on the right side and we should. Mounting on the left became popular when horses were used as military mounts in combat. Soldiers kept the swords or sabers on the left side of their horses, so it became a tradition to always mount on the left.

However, we've taken it much further. We tend to do everything on the left — halter, lead, bridle, saddle, mount and dismount, put on blankets, etc. Then we wonder why horses aren't good on the right. Make a point of spending more time on the right. It seems awkward at first because you're not used to it, but in time becomes easier.

## Get On!

Once you've determined he's thoroughly ready, mount again, and this time sit down carefully in the saddle. Don't hit it with a thud. Lower yourself into the seat purposely. Don't dilly-dally or creep up on him in

doing it, though. Mounting and dismounting are your most vulnerable times with any horse because that's when you're unseated. If your horse should spook or move suddenly, either step down to the ground or sit quickly in the saddle.

Once you're seated, put your feet all the way in the stirrups. Allow your horse to stand there. Don't ask him to move yet. A well-prepared horse will stand quietly, but there are no guarantees.

***Note:*** Don't mount or dismount a horse that's moving. I think this applies to any horse, even a well-broke one. When you get on or off a moving horse, you teach him a bad habit. Your horse should stand still until you ask him to move.

If your horse seems at all nervous during the mounting process, step down, tie the lead rope around the saddle horn, and send your horse around the corral a couple of times. Let him realize that there's no reason to be afraid. Bring him back and start over.

Another option to mounting an unsure, green horse is to do so from a steady saddle horse. Having another horse in the pen calms the colt and, with you above him, it

## A BETTER WAY

### Night Latch or Bucking Strap

A handy piece of equipment I have on every saddle is a night latch or bucking strap. It's a leather or nylon strap that buckles or fastens around the gullet of the saddle. It serves as a handhold when a horse bolts, bucks or jumps.

A horse can quickly snatch a saddle horn out of your hand, but you can hold on to a strap much easier. This simple strap has saved me countless times.

*A night latch gives a rider a chance to hold onto a bucking horse.*

*When preparing to mount an unsure horse from a saddle horse, perform all the mounting prep exercises, such as slapping the stirrup leathers against the horse's sides.*

*When the horse is ready, mount from the saddle horse. This method of mounting is for the advanced horseman.*

gives him a chance to see you in that position. He gets used to the idea before you mount and that helps his confidence level.

With the lead rope, bring the green horse fairly close to you and do all the mounting prep exercises mentioned above, such as rocking the saddle horn, slapping the stirrups against the horse's sides, etc.

When you think the green horse is ready, position him so it's easy for you to put your left foot in the left stirrup and slip onto his back from the saddle horse. Just sit there a while and let the green horse soak in the idea.

When you're mounted, stay relaxed but alert. Don't be nervous or scared because the horse can sense it.

What's the first thing you should do when you mount a green horse for the first time? Get off. Step down as carefully as you got up. Your horse will realize that you aren't a predator or stuck on his back forever.

As in mounting, prepare your horse for dismounting. Move around in the saddle a little bit, pat the horse's neck, rub his rump with your hand, simulating your leg brushing over the top.

The first thing you should do after mounting a green horse for the first time is get off! But prepare the horse for what's coming by moving around in the saddle as a signal and leaning to the left so he sees you in his left eye.

Step down rather quickly, being careful not to hit the horse's rump with your leg. Mounting and dismounting are two of the most dangerous times, because you're in a vulnerable position.

In the beginning, hold your lead rope short enough so that if the horse should buck, you could turn his head and maintain some control.

To change directions, slacken the lead rope and throw it over the horse's head as you did in the desensitizing exercises.

*Guide the horse the other way. Don't expect too much out of the first ride.*

*Try for a few steps backward by putting the lead rope around the base of the horse's neck. Ask him to back by tugging alternately or applying steady pressure on the rope and saying "back, back, back."*

You can dismount on either side. Your horse won't care, so do what's most comfortable for you. Before you dismount, however — for example, on the left — lean over and allow your horse to see you in his left eye. Don't surprise him; you want him to know you're there.

Then back your left boot out of the stirrup, but leave the tip of your toe in the stirrup. Remove your right boot completely from the right stirrup. Step down somewhat quickly toward the horse's left shoulder. Don't step toward the hindquarters in case your horse decides to kick. Pet or rub your horse to reassure him all is okay.

Mount again and this time pick up on the lead rope, but don't pull it. Have it short enough that if your horse starts bucking, you can turn his head toward you to make him stop. If this doesn't stop him, do your best to go with him until he quits. Your job is to be a passenger on your horse. This is the first ride, and you shouldn't expect too much from it. You want your horse to accept you and the saddle without fear.

Most well-prepared horses, however, stand there and don't know what to do. You'll have to create energy to get forward movement. Push him with your body; squeeze with your legs (but don't use your spurs at this point); cluck or make smooching sounds (he's used to them from earlier lessons); touch his rump with your free hand — anything that causes him to take a step forward.

If nothing works, you might have a friend enter the round pen and drive your horse off, just as you did during the ground-driving phase.

Once you get forward movement, go with your horse on a loose rope. Don't try to guide him yet. Make a few laps of the round pen.

When your horse seems relaxed, change directions, but do so with forward movement. Throw the rope over his head (as you did in ground work) and ask him to turn the other way.

You might even ask for a few steps backward, but be happy with even the slightest try. Place the rope around the base of the horse's neck. With short tugs and a verbal command of "back," ask the horse to take a step backward. The instant he does, stop tugging and reward him with release and a pat on the neck.

After you've ridden quietly in both directions and perhaps backed a few steps, get off your horse, loosen the cinches, and pet him to let him know he's done well.

The first ride should be a very positive experience. I think a lot of people underestimate the importance of the first ride to a horse, his first month and even first 6 months under saddle. That can set a precedent for the horse's entire life.

Your objectives for the first ride(s) are to develop the foundation for communication, feel, timing and balance between yourself and your horse. The goal is to take the fear out of your horse and cultivate trust.

## Direct or One-Rein Work

If, after several rides in the halter, you feel your horse is comfortable and relaxed, replace the rope halter with the rope hackamore. It's easy for the horse to understand guiding or "following a feel" in the hackamore because of the direct pull you get between the hackamore's noseband and reins. A rope hackamore is similar to a halter but it has a headstall, a soft rawhide noseband without a heel knot and two braided reins for simple and direct rein action. (See Chapter 5, "Equipment.")

In the beginning, do most all guiding using one rein. It's a mistake to use two reins so early in the game. Don't try to turn, stop or back your horse using two reins. All it does is confuse the horse. He can brace against the pull, throw his head up and keep moving his feet, which isn't the result you want.

One of the first things to teach your horse is flexibility, and you do that with one-rein

*After the halter and lead rope, graduate to a rope hackamore.*

*Test out the horse's guidance system on the ground first.*

*A quick release when the horse gives to rein pressure helps him understand what it's all about.*

*Bending is the primary means of controlling a green horse.*

work. Using one rein, bend your horse by leading or guiding the horse's head out to the side. You can do this on the ground first to check out the horse's response before you mount.

Once mounted, ask the horse for his head again. In this flexed position, find a holding spot where the horse's head is tipped comfortably at approximately a 90-degree angle to his body. If you can bend him, you can turn him. If you can turn him, you can stop him. Release pressure as soon as your horse gives to it. That's the way he learns to guide.

Never ride outside the round pen if your horse isn't bending well. You don't want to be at the mercy of any horse without some form of control. Bending is the primary method of getting control of your horse.

Think of your horse's hindquarters as his motor, engine or drive shaft. All movement and energy come from behind. When you bend or flex your horse's head around, his hind legs move laterally and that gives you control over his hindquarters. For example, when you bend your horse's head and neck to the left, his hindquarters move to the right and vice versa. This gives you control over the direction your horse travels.

Bending takes away the power from his engine. Because your horse simply moves in a small circle, you've taken away his drive, and that puts you back in control.

With your rope hackamore on your horse, trot or lope a few laps around the round pen. Then, change directions by going across the pen. Use your inside or direct rein to lead (don't pull back) your horse across into the middle. He should follow the feel of the direct rein on the hackamore nosepiece. When you come to the other side, your horse will naturally have to turn right or left, and that's when you guide him in the direction you want to go.

When you guide with the reins in your hands, do something with your legs, as well.

Many riders don't use their legs enough. Great riders do. Leg pressure is one of the best cue and communication systems you have.

At first, keep it simple and make it easy for your horse to understand. For example, if you're moving to the left, lead out with your left or direct rein (your horse will also see your hand in his left eye), open up your left leg (take it away from your horse's side) and press with your right leg. At the same time, lay your right rein across your horse's neck. This helps your horse turn left. Direct and support everything you do.

The supporting rein is a precursor to neck-reining. As time goes by, your hands will get closer together and you'll neck-rein your horse. But in the beginning, do everything with a direct rein.

To go to the right, lead with the direct, or in this case, right rein, open up your right leg and press your left leg into the horse's side as you lay the left supporting rein across his neck. Do this several times across the pen to accustom your horse to bending and following a feel of the reins.

Throughout this exercise your horse will learn two things: 1/ to follow the feel of the direct rein leading him in the direction of travel and 2/ to move away from leg pressure against his sides and the indirect rein against his neck. As soon as your horse responds, reward him by releasing both your rein and leg pressure.

## Out of the Round Pen

Once your horse gets a handle on bending and leading, it's time to get out of the round pen. He can become sour or lose enthusiasm with too much round-pen work.

Find places to go and something to do outside the confines of a pen or arena. Nearby trails are ideal.

The perfect situation would be to have an "escort rider" on an experienced horse. Your young horse will feel more comfortable because he's following one of his own kind, which makes him part of a little herd.

*When you're comfortable enough to venture outside the round pen, it helps to have an escort rider on a quiet, steady, experienced mount.*

On the trail, try some of the same exercises you did in the round pen. Bend your horse in a tight 360-degree circle and, as you drive out of it, still follow your companion. Bend your horse to a stop and say "whoa."

Most everything you do is still with one rein, turning right and left and stopping. In doing so, use your verbal cues to your advantage — smooch or cluck for forward movement, "whoa" for stopping and "back" for backing. Be consistent and your horse will remember his previous lessons.

By getting out of the pen or arena, you're training your horse in such a way that he doesn't even know he's being trained. He doesn't think of it as training; he thinks of it as getting to go places and do things. It's fun and exciting for him. In time, your horse will look forward to you riding him.

## Bits and Bridling

Your horse is ready to begin wearing a bridle at this point. But before you bridle him, make sure you can handle his muzzle. If your earlier desensitization lessons sank in, your horse should allow you to put your thumb into the sides of his mouth and even rub his tongue a little bit, and put your hand over his poll and rub his ears. Ideally, you should be able to put one hand on his poll and the other on the bridge of his nose and ask your horse to drop his head.

When first bridling a horse, introduce the bit as slowly and methodically as you did the saddle and pad.

Initially, have your rope hackamore on your horse's head. Over it, place a true snaffle bit, attached to a browband headstall

*To bridle, hold the top of the browband headstall in your right hand, part the horse's lips with your left thumb and wait for the horse to open his mouth. When he does, lift the headstall and slide the snaffle bit into his mouth.*

# HERE'S HOW

## Unbridling a Horse

Careful unbridling is as important as careful bridling. When you get in a hurry or rip the bit out of your horse's mouth, it makes him nervous or apprehensive because it's painful. This thoughtless act creates head-shyness and bridling problems.

I recommend the following:

1. Unbuckle the throatlatch first.

2. Pull the headstall over the left ear first, then the right. (You can use either hand, depending on the situation.)

3. Drop your hand slowly and instead of pulling the bit out of the horse's mouth, allow your horse to drop it himself.

Some horses hold the bit a moment or two. Always wait until a horse opens his mouth and lets go of the bit himself.

Remember, the true bridle horse carries the bit. To rip it out of his mouth is to undo the work you're trying to accomplish. Patience is waiting without worry.

*Unbridle as carefully as you bridle.*

with no reins. (See Chapter 5, "Equipment, Tools of the Horseman's Trade" for a description of a true snaffle bit.)

Use a curb (or chin) strap to hobble the snaffle rings together. Generally, the strap prevents the snaffle rings from being pulled through the horse's mouth when you apply rein pressure. Even though there are no reins in the early stages of bridling, I like to use the curb strap all the same.

At this point, your horse will learn to simply carry the snaffle in his mouth without any pressure from the reins.

To bridle, stand on your horse's left side, hold the top of the browband headstall in your right hand and cradle the snaffle bit between your left thumb and fingers. Place the bit underneath and behind your horse's muzzle. Stick your left thumb into the corners of your horse's mouth and move it back and forth.

When your horse opens his mouth, raise your right hand, which brings up the snaffle. Be patient with your horse. He'll eventually part his lips and, when he does, gently lift the bit and place it in his mouth. Adjust the headstall so that the snaffle rests at the corners of the horse's mouth. There shouldn't be a wrinkle or smile on your horse's lips. That's too tight.

Don't ever force the bit because, if you do, your horse will fight it and not accept it gracefully. He can become easily head-shy.

Slip the headstall over the right ear first, then the left. With the slack taken out of the headstall, slipping it over the left ear becomes easier. Lastly, buckle your throatlatch piece, but not too tightly, just enough to keep your horse from shaking off the bridle. Usually, two or three fingers-width is sufficient.

Ride your horse like this for a week or more to help him learn to carry the bit.

## Two Reins

Once he's comfortable with that, slowly introduce the snaffle-bit reins. Attach reins to the snaffle and ride with two sets of reins — those attached to the hackamore and those attached to the snaffle. Primarily, you'll use the hackamore reins at first, then slowly engage the snaffle reins in conjunction with the hackamore reins. Your horse will make the transference over time. From the hackamore reins, he'll learn to give with his nose, and from the snaffle reins, he'll learn to follow the feel in his mouth. This is called double- or two-reining.

All this is new to your horse so be patient and remember: Learning takes time.

## True Story:
## Perseverance —
## Riding the Tough Ones

People are curious and often ask, "What's the toughest horse you've ever worked?" "Has there ever been a horse you couldn't tame?" Traveling around the country as a horse trainer who'll work with any horse is much like a prizefighter willing to take on all comers.

I was a professional bull rider for many years and competed at the country's biggest rodeos. My challenge was to ride the rankest bulls the stock contractor could provide. In rodeo, it's the cowboy versus the contractor. The cowboy says, "I can ride anything you've got," and the contractor says, "I can put you on the ground."

When I began putting on public colt-starting demonstrations, I never meant them to be a challenge; however, my audience had other ideas. Instead of bringing horses for a learning demonstration, people brought them as a contest. "Craig Cameron is coming to town? Yeah, have we got one for him." After 20 years of proving myself and the method of working through understanding with horses, regrettably this contesting still goes on. I think it's a lot like auto racing or rodeo. Some folks come hoping to see a wreck.

Tough horses — I can name you a few. Las Cruces, N. M., 1992, a bad mare flipped completely over on me. Oklahoma City, a rank and spoiled stallion ran me over, and I still carry that scar on my shoulder today. At the Red Steagall Cowboy Gathering in Fort Worth, I was kicked to the ground. Amarillo Ranch Rodeo, I was kicked by an outlaw and had to be helped on the horse to finish before going to the hospital to drain the fluid off my knee. I was bucked off three times by the same mare in Ardmore, Okla., before finally "getting through" on that horse. Ask James Gholson, wagon boss of the Pitchfork Ranch, or the crowd that attended the Sweetwater, Texas, Ranch Rodeo about the black stallion that kicked me down, pawed me

and bucked me off twice before I "conquered" that bronc. The list goes on and on. Obviously, there've been many tough horses, but one in particular comes to mind when I think of truly tough.

My good friend, and one of the finest horsemen I know, Mark Chestnut of Whitesboro, Texas, had three long yearlings for sale, two fillies and a stallion. They were well-bred and the price was right. We sealed the deal, and my wife, Dalene, and I headed to Whitesboro. Not being halter-broke, the youngsters were wild but looked great. We crowded them into my stock trailer and were homeward bound with our new horses in tow.

The two fillies broke out soft and melted down into a smooth training routine. The little stallion that I eventually had gelded, however, was a horse of a different color. There was something contrary about him. He had a standoffish air. Just catching him in a stall was a task, even though he wore a halter and lead rope. He received many hours of leading, brushing, tying, and good ground work, but still the trust wasn't there.

My first trip to the round pen with this guy was memorable. The setting was an indoor arena with a 45-foot portable round pen set close to the barn window. I simply walked into the training corral. I hadn't moved or even started to work the young prospect when, without warning, he unhesitatingly and very athletically jumped completely out of that barn window and was gone. I think I laughed and cussed at the same time. I knew right then that this horse was a bit of a rattlesnake and was wild as sage. We started calling him Sage.

Sage got regular sessions in the round pen. He wasn't the type of horse you'd ever want to miss working on. I worked with him afoot, and I worked with him from other horses. I desensitized, sacked out and ponied him on a regular schedule, at least once a day and sometimes three sessions per day. This horse truly tested my patience more than any horse and most mules could. The way young Sage bucked with the first saddling, I knew he was an outlaw, but more importantly, I could see that he was a great athlete. That athleticism made me determined not to quit on this horse. I knew if I could get that athletic ability to work positively, instead of negatively, he'd be a great horse.

I had a young apprentice at the time named John Ross. John was all "cowboy" and was working hard to become a horseman. I think you needed to be both to deal with Sage. John and I'd take turns topping him out. He was the kind of horse that was no fun. Sage was dangerous. One of us would snub and the other would ride. It was tough going. If you could stay on Sage, your problems weren't over. He might settle down for a while, and then break in two again. Nerve-wracking was the way I think John put it. He was right, and these sessions were always long.

One more thing, getting off Sage was just as hard and as dangerous as getting on. If you've ever been on a horse you couldn't get off, then you know what I'm talking about. I'd lean over to get off and away Sage would go again. We used the rodeo pickup-man style of get-off or the just-jump-off-and-onto-the-fence-to-save-your-life type exit. On several occasions we discussed, where Sage could hear us, of course, getting rid of that S.O.B. Determination got the best of me, however, and I kept on.

Slowly, Sage improved. First bridling, first circles, first pasture ride — the slow process began to show some progress. It seemed Sage's job in life was to make everything hard. I must say, though, he did have natural talent. Great natural stops, turns and spins seemed effortless to Sage. In spite of the long, dark journey, a small light of hope began to break through. A year and a half came and went, and Sage became quite the item and topic of conversation at the ranch. Not totally trustworthy, by any means, Sage, in spite of himself, was getting good.

One afternoon one of the new apprentices spoke about Sage being hard-headed, hard-to-handle, ill-tempered and just plain old mean. Laughingly, Dalene said, "That sounds like Craig." Everyone howled and got a good laugh, but from that moment on Sage became "Craig."

Throughout the training process, I kept Mark Chestnut, my good "friend," abreast of this interesting horse. We had many good laughs and, needless to say, Mark pleaded innocent of any prior knowledge about Craig at the time of the sale. He did, however, say he wanted to ride him for a while.

Craig spent a whole year with Mark. In that time, Mark never sent even one bill. I kept telling him I'd come and pick up Craig, and he'd just laugh and say, "No." I'd ask how the horse was doing and he'd casually comment, "Oh, he's doing okay." I was never sure if he was riding him or what he was doing. Finally, I insisted that I'd better come and get him. When I got to his ranch, Mark surprised me with an incredible horsemanship demonstration of roping, cutting and reining skills on the outlaw Craig. What a great job Mark had done! Craig still snorted when approached, and Mark had to admit that he still couldn't get him shod. In an unguarded moment, Craig had even bucked off Mark once. But Craig was the athlete I knew he could be.

I now do colt-breaking, reining, and cutting demonstrations on this amazing horse. The crowds love him. Still, he has an unbelievable sense of self-preservation about him. That's what makes him unique and, in some ways, I think that's what I like about him most. I always say the toughest horses teach you the most. It's raw horsemanship and that takes lots of desire, determination and dedication on the part of the horseman.

When last I talked to John Ross, he asked me if Craig was still tough. I told him, "Yeah, he's still more than a little snorty."

**Editor's Note:** The horse Craig is shown riding on the cover of this book (as well as in many chapters) is Craig, the former outlaw.

*"Without flexibility there's no position and without position, there's no control of the horse."*

# 15

# BASIC FLEXIBILITY EXERCISES

Flexibility in horses is fundamental in every discipline of horsemanship. It's through flexibility that you have control over your horse. It allows you to position his body, whether it's to a jump, a barrel, a cow, a gate or even a mailbox.

Flexibility begins with lateral flexion or the ability to bend the horse's body with one rein. A lot of horsemanship entails using one rein at a time. The last thing you want to do, especially with a young horse in the beginning, is pull with both reins. If you pull on the horse's mouth or head, his natural instinct is to pull back, whether you're on the ground or on his back.

By using one rein at a time, it's harder for your horse to brace or lean against you. Just hold your pressure until he finds the release point in giving. Then he learns to give instead of pull back. That's what your aids — hands, legs, bit, halter and lead rope, reins and spurs — are all about. Your horse learns to yield to the pressure you place upon him with these aids.

## Lateral Flexion

Lateral flexion is one of the first things to achieve with your horse because it's the basis for control. By bending your horse right and left with a single rein, you control where his body goes. Here's how to accomplish that.

*Flexibility is the prerequisite to performance.*

*To teach your horse to flex laterally, pick up one rein and hold with steady pressure.*

*The instant your horse gives his head, release your hold. Give back to the horse when he gives to you.*

First, outfit your horse with a side-pull or snaffle bit because they work off a direct pull on either the sides of the horse's face or the corners of his mouth. That makes it easy for the horse to follow the pressure; thus they're best for communicating lateral flexion. Shanked bits, on the other hand, apply too much pressure on a green horse who's trying to learn.

Pick up one rein, and hold it steady; don't pull on it. Learn the difference between holding and pulling. In holding the rein, you wait on the horse to respond. In pulling backward on the rein, you try to force the horse to respond with a tug-of-war technique.

One of the most important things in horsemanship is to never allow a horse to pull on your hands. If you let the reins slide through your hands, or your arm moves forward as the horse pulls, you've taught your horse to pull against pressure. Before you know it, to find release, he roots his nose in the air or pulls on your hands at your slightest rein cue.

As you pick up and hold the rein, wait on the horse to give his face. The second he does, release the pressure.

The amount of bend your horse gives isn't as important as the try he makes in giving it. Some horses resist more, but others give their heads easily. With a resistant horse, you might have to ask for more bend by bumping or shaking the bit until you can find a good spot to hold. Adjust to fit your particular situation and circumstance.

In the beginning, your horse might bend his body and walk around in a tight circle following the rein pressure. As he does, sit there, don't move in the saddle or use any leg pressure. When he finally stops, release your rein pressure.

Always be in control. Don't allow your horse to assume anything. In other words, if you want him to walk, cue him to walk. If, in the beginning, your horse walks around in response to a rein hold, just sit; make sure your legs aren't active and you're not moving with the horse. As soon as he stops, release. Your horse looks for the release. When he stops and you release him, he associates your hold with bending and flexing while standing still. That's the connection you want.

## Control the Hindquarters

Once you can flex your horse laterally and he gives his head right and left willingly and easily, then control and move the hindquarters with added leg pressure.

For instance, ask for lateral flexion to the right by tipping your horse's nose to the right. Place your right foot behind the cinch and look at the hindquarters where your foot is. Then, press or push the hindquarters over to the left. Make sure you leave slack in the left rein and don't use any left-leg pressure.

Use the same, but opposite cues, for controlling and moving the horse's hindquarters to the right. Tip your horse's nose to the left, place your left foot behind the cinch, look at your horse's left hindquarters and press or push the hindquarters to the right with your left leg. Keep your right rein and leg still. This is a turn on the forehand.

Remember, a lot of what you do with your hands and legs is a give-and-take motion. As

soon as your horse responds by giving his head and hindquarters, release your pressure and give back to the horse.

Throughout a 360-degree turn on the forehand, for example, don't continually hold your rein or leg pressure, but bump your horse every so often with your leg to remind him you want him to continue to turn.

I like to say, "If I'm doing something with my hands, I'm doing something with my legs, as well." Your hands and legs work in unison. Coordinate your movements with the horse's response. As he

*In a 360-degree turn on the forehand, a horse pivots around his relatively stationary front legs.*

# A BETTER WAY

### Flex-Test

In preparing to mount any strange horse, check out his rein response from the ground first. Make sure you can bend or flex his head and neck from side to side and that he backs a few steps when you pull back with both reins. If he can't do it on the ground, there's a good chance he won't do it with you in the saddle either. He doesn't have much of a steering mechanism and could even go over backward when you apply rein pressure. Such a horse needs to return to foundation or beginning work.

*Test out a strange horse's rein responses by seeing if the horse will give his head from side to side.*

turns, release your pressure. If he stalls out in the turn, gently bump him with the rein and your leg again.

In a 360-degree turn on the forehand, your horse performs a front-end pivot. His front legs are relatively stationary and his hind legs move around them. It's the most natural pivot for a horse to make because a horse carries most of his weight on the front end.

It all boils down to controlling the whole horse — head, neck, shoulders, rib cage, hindquarters and down to the feet.

These flexibility exercises (lateral flexion and control of the hindquarters) are so important because they're truly the basics, the fundamentals upon which you'll build your entire horsemanship and training program.

If at any time in training, your horse gets nervous or unsure of himself, stop what you're doing and go back to these exercises. They'll calm your horse and bring him back to an atmosphere of understanding. It's as if he says to himself, "Yes, I remember this; everything's okay."

*To move the forehand to the left, open up your left rein and open up (or take away) your left leg. Apply pressure with your right rein and leg.*

It's not only a physical thing, it's also a mental thing. It allows you to gain control of your whole horse — his body and his mind.

Should your horse ever become frightened and run away, you can control him with one rein. Pulling on two reins won't always stop your horse, especially if he's green or inexperienced. He'll brace against the reins, his head will go higher and his feet will go faster.

But if you can bend him with one rein, you can turn him; if you can turn him, you can stop him. Why? Because you control his hindquarters. A horse drives from behind, turns on his center and pulls with his front. If you control the hindquarters, you can control the whole horse.

## Control the Forehand

After moving the hindquarters around the front end, follow through with having the front end move around the hind end.

To do that to the left, pick up your left rein and move it out to the left in the direction you're headed. Apply slight neck pressure with your right or indirect rein and leg pressure with your right leg. Take your left leg away from your horse's side to open a doorway for him to move through.

To move to the right, extend your right rein to the right and place your left rein against the horse's neck. Remove any leg pressure from your horse's right side and apply light leg pressure on his left side.

In the beginning, perform this maneuver slowly one step at a time. Build a foundation so your horse understands where to place his feet.

*To move the forehand to the left, apply right rein pressure on the horse's neck and right leg pressure on his side.*

*To move the forehand to the right, open up your right rein and right leg and use left rein and leg pressure.*

## True Story: Death Grip

I think people underestimate the importance of flexibility in the horse. Trying to guide a horse without flexibility is like trying to drive a car with a steering wheel that doesn't turn. It just won't go where you want him to go.

At one of my clinics, a girl started the morning with a death grip on her horse's reins. The more she pulled, the more excited the horse became. Trying to escape the relentless pressure and pain, the horse did what instinct told him and that was to run.

As the girl pulled harder, the horse's head went higher and his feet went faster. Fortunately, the horse stopped in a corner of the pasture.

This horse, like all horses, needed to know how to bend, flex and give to pressure.

*"In true collection, there's a weight transfer from the front end to the engaged hindquarters."*

# 16

# FORWARD MOVEMENT AND COLLECTION

As I've said before, the one thing you must have to train any horse is forward movement. Nothing happens without this essential ingredient.

Just as in the lateral flexion exercises, the forward-movement exercises I describe below further teach your horse to yield to pressure, follow his nose, follow a feel, turn right and left and rate his speed. They allow you to really work with direct and indirect rein pressure.

## North-South-East-West Exercise

I like to call this exercise North-South-East-West because those are all the directions you go when you perform it.

Place eight cones (in pairs of two) in a circle on a level patch of ground, either in an arena or a pasture. I like to use cones because the horse can see them and understand the reason behind the turns you ask him to make. (See diagram, "North-South-East-West Exercise.")

There's no set pattern to this exercise. But one of the keys to horsemanship is knowing where you're going before you ever ask it of the horse. This exercise will tell on you if you don't know where you're going. You can't make last-minute decisions because then the horse is open to lots of mistakes. So know where you're going before you get there. Think

*A horse moving forward willingly and freely is critical to any training.*

# North-South-East-West Exercise

A. Start in the middle.
B. Ride through the North gate.
C. Ride through the East gate.
D. Ride through the West gate.
E. Ride through the South gate.
F. Ride through the North gate.
G. Ride through the West gate.
H. Ride through the East gate.
I. Ride through the South gate.

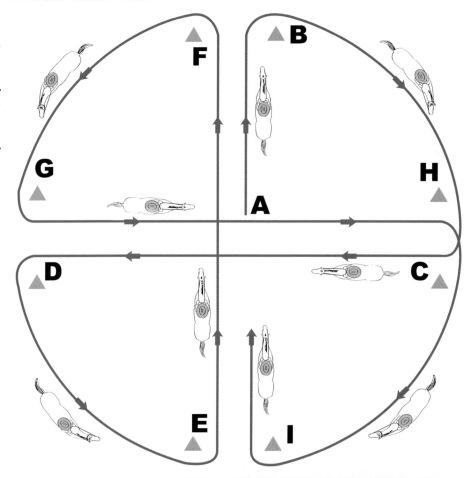

*Enter or exit the circle only between the gates formed by the cones.*

ahead. Form that habit as you work with your horse.

In this exercise, you can enter or leave the circle only through the four imaginary north, south, east and west gates formed by the cones.

Establish a pace or rhythm and ride through the cones, turning right and left through the gates as you go. Crisscross through the middle around the cones north, south, east and west. To add variety, circle your horse, say by going from the south gate through the west gate or north gate and then through the east gate.

Work first at a walk, then the trot. (The trot is your real working gait.) This is a great exercise to learn to move with your horse. The best riders I know ride with the last 6 inches of their spine. By that I mean their seat is in rhythm with their horse. You're not sitting on the horse, you're moving with him. You're not making him do all the work. You're actively riding and guiding him with your hands, seat and legs.

Place your hands in a working position in front (about 6 inches) of the saddle horn — not behind it or way out down the horse's

*Place your hands 6 inches in front of the saddle horn.*

mane. Keep your hands low. Remember, low hands, low head.

Also, don't lean into the turns by dropping your shoulders into them. That unbalances your horse and causes him to lean into them as well. Sit straight and in the middle of the saddle to maintain good balance.

*Don't lean into the turns. Sit straight in the saddle.*

## Direct-Rein Hand and Leg Coordination

*Your hands and legs work together in guiding the horse with direct and supporting aids. The cues are exaggerated here for illustration purposes, although in the beginning you might have to exaggerate before you can refine.*

*1. To direct rein to the left, open your left rein and left leg. Lay your supporting right rein against your horse's neck and your supporting right leg against his side.*

*3. To direct rein to the right, open your right rein and right leg. Lay your supporting left rein against your horse's neck and your supporting left leg against his side.*

*2. A direct rein to the left as seen from the back, with supporting right leg and right rein.*

*4. A direct rein to the right as seen from the back, with a supporting left leg and left rein.*

Direct rein as you move through the cones by leading with the rein in the direction you want to go. Literally, pick up the rein and move it out in the direction of travel. In the beginning, you might have to exaggerate as you teach your horse. Someday, you'll be able to refine your hand movements and rein one-handed. But for now, on a young or problem horse use both hands to direct rein through the cones.

For example, in asking your horse to turn right, lead out with the right rein. He should follow your suggestion and turn right around a cone. Support the leading right rein by laying the left rein on the horse's neck. In this case, your right rein is your leading rein and your left rein is your supporting rein.

Remember, your legs do what your hands do. If you lead out with your right rein, open up your right leg by taking it away from your horse's body. Support this by laying the outside or left rein against his neck and placing your left leg on his body. Throughout this exercise, your horse is giving and yielding to rein and leg pressure.

Guide him through the cones with right and left turns. While there's no set pattern to the turns, know where you plan to turn next as I said earlier. Soon, you'll develop a rhythm or tempo and your horse will begin to "turn loose," get soft throughout his entire body (head, neck, rib cage and hindquarters) and in tune with your cues.

## Weaving Exercise

This is essentially the same exercise as the North-South-East-West exercise, but the pattern gets tighter. Start out at a walk and graduate to a trot.

Now, instead of going through imaginary gates, weave through the cones. In this exercise your horse really has to follow the leader — you. Because the guiding rein and leg cues happen faster, they really help you teach your horse neck-reining (where the horse follows the supporting rein on his neck). It doesn't matter if you hit a cone;

*Weave through the cones, using the same direct-rein cues you use in the North-South-East-West exercise, although now the turns are tighter.*

the important thing is that you guide your horse through them.

Your cues are the same as in the North-South- East-West exercise. It's an opening and a closing. You open up with your right rein and right leg as you go to the right, closing your left rein and leg at the same time. In going to the left, you open up with your left rein and left leg and close with your right rein and right leg.

To vary the exercise, pick one cone and turn around it completely, either once or several times, really softening up and rounding out your horse's body as you bend his head, neck, rib cage and hindquarters around the cone. From this you can change directions and go the opposite way by just not completing the circle around the cone.

To side-pass to the right, tip your horse's nose to the left, open up your right leg and lay your left rein and leg against the horse.

To side-pass to the left, tip your horse's nose to the right, open up your left leg and lay your right rein and leg against your horse.

## Side-Passing Exercise

When you progress in the weaving exercise, you can actually get your horse to move laterally through the cones, also called side-passing or leg-yielding. You use slight forward movement here, but you can take advantage of the fact that it's a natural progression of the weaving exercise and a wonderful opportunity to teach your horse an advanced maneuver.

Unlike the previous exercise where you tip your horse's nose in the direction of travel, it's easiest for your horse to side-pass by tipping his nose away, which opens up his shoulder on the side you want to move toward.

For example, to side-pass to the right in between the cones, tip your horse's nose slightly to the left, thus opening up his right shoulder, freeing it to move to the right. This is one case, at least in the beginning, when

you might lean slightly to the left, rather than sit up straight. Lay your left rein on your horse's neck, press your left leg into his side and hold until your horse moves across the cone laterally. Do the opposite for side-passing to the left.

It doesn't matter if you miss a gate or cone, work for position, work to get ready for the next move. If things get too tight or close, pass by the cone and start again farther down the line.

One reason you introduce side-passing during the cone exercise is that your horse can see the cones; he sees the reason why you're asking him to move sideways. Remember, ask for only a step or two. Your horse doesn't have to side-pass all the cones. Be happy with a few steps in that direction and build upon that in the days and weeks to come.

## Collection

One of the keys in horsemanship is to get your horse working off the bit in a collected manner. That makes all performance possible and easier.

In my discussion of the mechanics of the horse (Chapter 3), I talked about the fact that a horse naturally carries most of his weight on his front end, about 60 percent. But performance work is done mostly on the hindquarters. Now we put a saddle and a rider up on the horse's back and even more weight ends up on the front end. It's no wonder horses stop on their front ends and easy to see why hindquarter maneuvers and pivots could be difficult for them.

Allowing a horse to work more off his hindquarters is what collection helps you achieve. Collection balances the horse's weight on all four feet and is also called "even-loading." When so balanced, a horse is more capable of performing a correct stop, back, spin and so on.

Collection isn't just about a horse dropping his head into the bit. Most mammals have seven vertebrae in their necks. The first two in the horse's poll region are the atlas and axis, and that's where you want a horse to hinge or to give his head. Actually, in perfect collection the horse's poll would be slightly higher than the withers, with the horse's nose in a vertical position. We often refer to this as "breaking at the poll." That rounds out the horse's spine, elevates the shoulders and back and puts more weight on the hindquarters, where the performance

*This horse is breaking nicely at the poll. Notice how he's giving his head in the bridle and that his poll is slightly higher than his withers.*

*This horse is over-bridled or over-bent at the poll, which is actually lower than his withers. In this position, the horse can be heavy on the forehand and unable to use his back properly.*

## HERE'S HOW

### A "Rocking" Cue

Another cue to collect your horse instead of a steady pull or hold with your hands, which can make him heavy, is to signal your horse with a soft, rocking motion of the bit. To accomplish this, alternately open and close your hands on the reins with a slight wrist movement. This creates a soft and light cue that encourages the horse to collect willingly. You can use this helpful cue at a walk, trot and canter.

horse works. In true collection, there's a weight transfer from the front end to the engaged hindquarters.

This is where a horse's conformation comes into play quite a bit. A horse with correct conformation finds it easier to break at the poll and to balance his entire body. A horse whose neck isn't built properly (ewe neck or upside-down curvature) finds it much more difficult if not impossible to become collected. Horses with short, heavy necks, thick at the throatlatch, have a much harder time breaking at the poll and, therefore, collecting. Also, horses with straight shoulders, long backs and high or straight hocks all have a harder time collecting than horses with good conformation.

To ask for collection, drive your horse into the bit by squeezing with your legs at the same time you pick up on the reins. Wait for your horse to drop his head or break at the poll. In the beginning, your

*This filly has the type of neck conformation and throatlatch that makes it easy for her to break at the poll.*

*Working at a trot, this horse is bridled up with good hindquarters engagement.*

*Even on a loose rein, this horse is collected. Notice that he's breaking slightly at the poll, his shoulders are elevated and his hindquarters are driving deeply underneath him.*

horse might raise his head in response to pressure from the bit or he might turn one way or the other searching for release. Hold the reins and wait for him to find it by dropping his head or breaking at the poll. The instant he does, immediately release. Start from a stop, then advance to a walk, progressing to the trot and then finally the canter. In time, he'll carry this longer and farther. He'll carry this "feel" that someday you'll call collection.

Eventually, when you squeeze your legs around your horse, your horse will "bridle up" and not speed up. With this squeeze the horse's nose will come down, and the horse should break at the poll. This squeeze isn't a cue to go faster; that's a whole different feel. The cue to speed up is to push with your body and seat. That tells the horse to speed up, but squeezing your legs around his rib cage is the cue to drop his head and, in doing so, raise his back or spine, which is all part of collection.

It's not the head going down that achieves the balance, it's the shoulders coming up. The top line of the spine, which includes the neck, shoulders and back, literally lifts. It lifts as the horse breaks at the poll. When it does, the horse's weight shifts backward, and he stands balanced on all four legs.

## A BETTER WAY

### You've Got Legs

If people used their legs as much as they use their hands, they'd be much better riders. Your hands are for guiding and positioning your horse, while your legs are for movement. With a conscientious effort to incorporate your legs, you'll find your horse will be better and more responsive.

In walking, trotting and cantering your horse, learn how to take hold or "hug" your horse with your legs. Instead of just kicking with your feet, learn to guide and push with your legs. For example, in legging a horse around a turn, squeeze with your entire leg, from your ankle to your seat bones. When the turn is complete, release your leg just as you'd release with your hands. Strong riders have strong legs.

The roundness on top comes from the neck breaking at the poll, the spine rounding and, consequently, the hindquarters dropping. When they do, they get more power to drive from behind and propel the horse forward in a balanced position.

When you collect your horse, you get the position you need for high-performance maneuvers. In everything you do with a horse, prepare first. Ready him first, then position him. In other words, before you stop your horse, position him for the stop. The correct position is for the horse to break at the poll in response to bit pressure, get round on top, elevate his front end and his back, then drop and engage his hindquarters.

With collection, you have a true bridle horse. When you pick up the reins, the bridle horse feels the pressure, and the first thing he does is break at the poll. You won't need a tie-down. Your horse's head will go down and he'll position himself for the maneuvers. Through repetition, your horse learns what he lives, and he lives what he learns. In the beginning, you'll have to exaggerate, but if he does it the correct way enough times, you can refine it as you go along. Someday, you won't have to work so hard at it. You'll pick up on the reins and your horse will respond instantaneously. You'll be able to develop good stops and spins through collection.

*Walk forward, tip your horse's nose to the left. You can use a fence or rail to help keep your horse straight.*

*Teach your horse to walk forward with his nose tipped both directions. Here, the horse's nose is tipped to the right. Use the left rein as a supporting rein.*

## Develop the Top Line

To develop softness in a horse, softness to the bit and to your leg, start at a walk (later progress to faster gaits), pick up on a rein, say the right rein, and ask your horse to slightly tip his nose to the right as you walk straight ahead. Use your supporting or off rein softly and straight back for flexion, speed and direction. Your horse should drop his nose and collect himself. He learns to travel in a forward movement broke at the poll and with his nose slightly tipped right. In the beginning, you instantaneously release when he gives, but in time he'll hold this position longer and longer. Go 10 yards at first, then 20, then 30, and your horse will hold the softness or lightness in the bridle as you walk along. His nose will be tipped, but he'll walk straight forward. Then, tip the nose to the left and do the same thing.

This exercise develops the top line with flexion and position for a correct framework. Your horse gets stronger and stronger in his top line, which is where the lift for collection comes from. His musculature gets stronger. There's a ligament across the top of his neck that develops with this exercise.

It's just as if you were working out at a gym. In the beginning, your muscles tire quickly, but as time goes on and you continue exercising, you get stronger and stronger and can go longer and longer in your workout. It's the same for a horse and his physical structure. Teaching your horse to travel in a collected manner should be a slow and methodical process.

In every exercise you do, even circling or going through the forward-movement exercises such as the North-South-East-West exercise, have your horse begin to work collected. It's all part of the puzzle. You won't get one without the other. They begin to fit together. It's all preparation, positioning and framework. All the exercises fit together to help the horse hold his frame in a collected manner.

The historic European horse masters knew collection is the key to great horsemanship, and the greatest trainers in the world today don't omit these steps.

## True Story: A Ride with Jake

*On a beautiful day in the fall of 1996, a young man named John Ross and I rode our colts around my Double Horn Ranch. We were in dense woods, the day was cool and overcast with fall leaves covering the trail, making rustling noises as we moved through them.*

*I had John's 5-year-old son Jake riding double with me on a young gelding that John said was gentle. The trail wound its way to the top of a bluff overlooking the Paluxy River. The river ran cool and slow about 25 feet below us. The path then headed in a slow but gradual upward angle.*

*With John riding ahead of us, Jake and I started to negotiate the small incline at a steady pace on our young steed. For no good reason, the gelding stopped. I waited a moment before trying to urge him forward and that's when the trouble started. This unpredictable horse began going backward.*

*Trying to maintain calm, I urged him forward. No luck and no forward movement. It didn't take an experienced hand to realize that this was a problem. With the bluff and river behind me, Jake in front of me and a green horse under me, going in reverse was trouble with a capital "T." No urging, spurring, smooching or any other cue changed the direction of this horse, which was reverse. All three of us went over the bluff into midair. I grabbed Jake and kicked away from the horse. All three of us landed in the river with a tremendous splash. I guess the angels rode with us because we all landed unscathed. The horse and Jake were wide-eyed, but miraculously unhurt.*

*This dramatic story emphasizes the importance of forward movement. It was a lack of forward movement that got us in trouble. As we shook ourselves off, I asked tough little Jake if he would like to ride out of the river bottom with me. He pulled down his hat, looked up at me and in his best 5-year-old fashion said, "No, I think I'll walk."*

# 17
# CIRCLES AND LEAD CHANGES

Circles are basic to any training program, and they're the foundation of most upper-level riding maneuvers. Your horse learns to accept your guidance and control and to rate his speed through large, fast circles and small, slow ones. He also learns preparation for lead changes.

Circles are great tattletales. They tell on you and how well you've trained your horse. It's obvious in a circle if your horse is paying attention to you. He should be upright and balanced and drive from behind. His circle either stays round and the horse moves at a steady pace, or the circle is ragged and the horse's movement is uneven.

## Performing Perfect Circles

To ride a perfect circle, first find a center point around which you can ride. It can be a cone, barrel, post, bush or rock, but select some stationary object to circle around. You'll know you're riding perfect circles when you stay the same distance from that center point as you move around it.

At first, maintain a trot around the center point. When you feel your horse relaxes and is ready to lope or canter, gently lift the inside rein and press or cue with outside leg pressure. Ideally, cue with your hand and leg at the same time. See how little pressure it takes for your horse to respond. If you need to, you also can encourage a lope by using verbal cues, such as smooching or clucking, whatever it takes to get into a lope. If your horse still won't go, then bump him with your outside leg. Don't forget to push with your seat

*Large or small, fast or slow, a good circle is round and the horse maintains a steady pace.*

*Find a center point around which to circle. Start out at a trot and graduate to a canter.*

*At a canter, maintain the same distance around the center point.*

bones. You could even reach back with your hands or reins and lightly tap his outside hip.

Notice your horse's body position at the lope. It should be the same shape as the circle — round from the tip of your horse's nose to his hindquarters. If you're in a right circle, your horse should be on a right lead. His right front leg leads the other three.

Also, notice your own body position. In a right circle your right shoulder and leg are slightly ahead of your left shoulder and left leg. The converse is true in a left circle, when your left shoulder and left leg are slightly ahead of your right shoulder and right leg. This is natural and means you're in rhythm or sync with your horse. To stay balanced while riding circles, ride the center of your horse. However, you might find that you have to put more weight in your outside stirrup to stay balanced in a circle.

At the canter, sit quietly, don't push your horse to go faster by urging him on with your seat. The faster you move, the faster he'll go. There's an art to just sitting at the canter and even sitting slightly slower than your horse is going. That allows your horse to find your rhythm and rate his pace to match yours.

Also, make sure your body isn't leaning into the circle. Instead, sit up straight. If you lean, your horse will lean into the circle, too. In time, it becomes a habit. Leaning to the inside makes it hard for him to perform lead changes correctly. Your horse should be balanced on all four feet.

Even if you're not leaning, your horse might be. Typically, the problem is that he drops his shoulder into the circle. When he does, block it by bumping your horse lightly with your inside rein and leg. Do this by making light contact with the inside rein in an upward motion. At the same time, bump your inside leg at the cinch to encourage him to lift the shoulder and rib cage.

It's crucial that your horse be "broke" to your leg, meaning he responds to leg pressure on his side or rib cage. Desensitize your horse enough that you can put your leg on him without it spooking or bothering him. If you've done the desensitization exercises mentioned in earlier chapters, then this shouldn't be a big problem.

If your horse tries to drift to the outside of the circle and go wider, build a wall with your outside rein and outside leg, laying both on your horse. Put your outside leg slightly back on his side and push the hindquarters into the circle. Keep his neck and nose somewhat straight and the shoulder vertical with light upward pressure with your inside rein. Use a combination of right and left rein to keep your horse straight on the circle's path.

By now you know that you should instantly release the second your horse responds to your rein and leg cues. Even if you know your horse is going to be wrong the next step, still turn the horse loose. Someday, he'll learn to carry the "good feel," the correctness, farther and farther on his own, which is a form of "self-carriage."

As your horse canters around the cones, learn to guide him. Make little "fixes," then release. If you find you have to pull on your horse, you're not ready for the canter. Go back to the trot. Stay in control until you feel your horse understands how to guide at the canter.

## Lead Departures

Correct lead departures come from hindquarter control or the ability to move the hindquarters one direction or the other. (See Chapter 15, "Basic Flexibility Exercises.") This lateral movement away from leg pressure is the key to correct canter or lead departures.

Start at a walk. When the horse is straight, give the leg cue to canter. For example, for a left lead departure, start by walking your horse straight ahead. Simultaneously, lift your hands, the left hand slightly higher than the right, and squeeze with your right leg behind the cinch. At the same time, you could push with your seat bones and use a verbal cue, such as smooching or clucking. If your horse understands lateral movement with his hindquarters, he'll strike off straight and in a left lead. Do just the opposite for a right lead.

Good lead departures are the key for correct lead changes.

*A horse strikes off into a lead departure by propelling himself from the hindquarters.*

## Lead Changes

In lead changes, the horse switches leads from right to left or left to right at the rider's command. It's a phase-sequence of footfalls in which the hind legs interchange their roles. If you're going to the left, your horse should be in his left lead and vice versa. It's important to know where your horse's feet are at all times, especially when asking for performance maneuvers, such as lead changes. Get in rhythm with your horse's feet.

The main problem most people have in changing leads is that they don't have a lead-change language to help their horse; the horse lacks the foundation exercises necessary to accomplish this maneuver. Go back to the basics before you attempt to change leads on your horse. Make sure he understands the flexion and forward movement exercises first. It's a prerequisite that he's able to move his hindquarters around his front end (turn on the forehand). Don't attempt lead changes until your horse can perform nice circles on a loose rein.

Horses trot in a diagonal gait. In other words, the left front and right rear move together and the right front and left rear move simultaneously. When you post the trot, you do so on a particular diagonal. When circling to the left with the arena wall on your right, you'd rise and fall with the right front foot, which means the left rear as well. You're in the correct rhythm with the horse to take the left lead because that diagonal doesn't change.

## A BETTER WAY

### Crossfiring or Cross-Cantering

Sometimes a horse lopes in one lead in front and another behind — called crossfiring. It's not a particularly athletic movement, and the horse is neither balanced nor moving correctly when he does it. It's really rough to ride, and you'll know when it happens.

To correct this, simply speed up your horse. Ask him to move out faster until he makes the change. The speed encourages him to synchronize his hindquarters with his front end, at which point he'll move in a true three-beat canter.

There's a diagonal in the three-beat canter or lope as well, as I explained in Chapter 3 "Mechanics of the Horse." In a left lead, the diagonal would be the left hind leg and the right front leg moving together. The footfall sequence for a left lead would be: Beat one: The horse pushes off with his right rear leg. Beat two: The left rear leg and right front leg move together, which is the diagonal pair. Beat three: Finally, the left front leg follows, which is the leading leg. There's an airborne phase before the right rear strikes the ground again and starts the sequence all over.

In a right lead, beat one is the left rear leg pushing off. Beat two is the right rear leg moving with the left front leg, which is the diagonal pair. Finally, in beat three the right front leg follows, which is the leading leg. Again, there's an airborne phase before the left rear leg starts the sequence all over.

## Drop-to-the-Trot and Flying Lead Changes

You can teach your horse to change leads through various means. One of the easiest ways is with a direction change, but they also can be taught in a straight line. Lead changes aren't direction changes; however, in the early stages of teaching them, the direction change physically helps your horse understand why and what you're attempting to do.

In the drop-to-the-trot (sometimes called simple lead changes) exercise, you'll use a combination of straight lines and direction changes to make it easy for the horse to change leads.

The North-South-East-West pattern (See Chapter 16, "Forward Movement and Collection.") or a large circle is good for teaching drop-to-the-trot lead changes. Think of the circle in the shape of the letter "D," which has a straightaway where the drops-to-the-trot and lead changes occur. (See "D-Shaped Circle" diagram.)

For example, when circling to the left in a left lead, prepare for a lead change by coming across the middle or straightaway of

# D-Shaped Circle Exercise

A. Circle in left lead.
B. Drop to the trot across the middle or straightaway, which makes the "circle D-shape."
C. Cue for right lead.
D. Circle in right lead.
E. Come across middle or straightaway and drop to the trot again.
F. Cue for left lead.

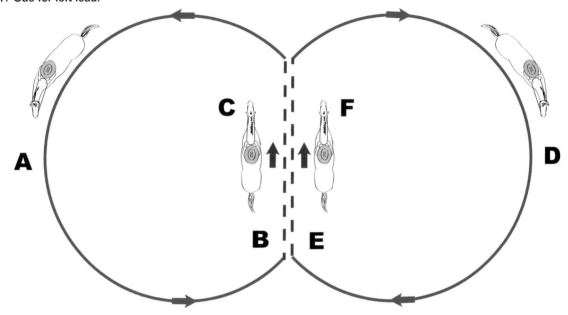

# HERE'S HOW

## Circle Within a Circle

The Circle Within a Circle pattern involves big and small circles and is an excellent exercise to promote correct leads and control. (While this exercise is described at the canter, it's not a bad idea to start at a trot, then work up to a canter.)

1. Set up two 50-gallon drums or barrels along the perimeter of a large circle, opposite one another.

2. Canter a large circle to the left.

3. Without changing gait, make a small circle around one of the barrels and then return to the large circle.

4. It's not necessary to circle a barrel each time you approach one.

5. Every so often, incorporate a small circle around the barrel and then return to the larger circle.

6. Be creative and sometimes circle the barrel two or three times before you return to the larger circle.

7. Make direction and lead changes by coming across the middle of the circle.

*The Circle Within a Circle exercise helps teach leads and control.*

the circle. In the beginning it's easiest to drop to the trot prior to asking for a lead change. Slow your body and softly pull on the reins as cues to transition to a trot.

When your horse trots, immediately cue him to strike off on the right lead. Remember the cue for changing him from a left to right lead is to gently lift on the reins, the right rein slightly higher than the left, and at the same moment, press or bump with the left leg. Lifting on the reins elevates the horse's shoulder or front end.

The lead change should take place on the straightaway across the circle. Once the lead change has occurred, resume your circle in the opposite direction, which would be to the right on a right lead. Allow your horse to slow down, relax and become quiet. Don't rush the lead-change process.

When your horse feels soft, prepare for another change. This time make it from right to left. While circling to the right, guide your horse across the middle of the circle. When your horse is straight, slow your body and transition from the canter to a trot. Immediately cue your horse to take the left lead by lifting the reins, the left hand slightly higher than the right, and bumping or pressing with your right leg while still maintaining your rein position. Your horse should move from trot to

canter and now be in the left lead. As you complete the straightaway across the middle of the circle on a left lead, turn to the left.

Lead changes at a canter take place when the horse is airborne or in suspension. That's why it's called a "flying" lead change. Perform flying lead changes by using the same body position as required for the drop-to-the-trot lead changes, but maintain a canter throughout the process.

Don't overdo lead-change work. Get a few changes and quit for the day. Remember, the essential ingredients for good lead changes are the basics — hindquarter control, lead departures, good loose-rein circles, collection and straightness.

## Figure-Eight X Exercise

As you and your horse get better at lead changes, try the Figure-Eight X exercise. In this pattern, you make your changes in the middle of the arena on a straightaway, not using a radical direction change as you did in the D-shaped circle.

The figure-eight pattern has a large X in the middle, which provides the long straightaways for lead departures, drop-to-trot lead changes and flying lead changes. (See "Figure-Eight X" diagram.)

### True Story: Naturally Leaded

*Leads are natural to a horse. However, some horses are better at changing leads than others.*

*On several occasions I witnessed horses that were traveling on the wrong lead or didn't make a lead change after changing directions. They ended up taking some big falls.*

*One time at a working cow horse event, I saw a horse and rider taking a cow down the fence at a high rate of speed. When the cow changed directions, the horse followed without*

*changing leads. In this unbalanced position, the horse went head-over-heels and rolled over the rider. The horse wasn't hurt, but the man had to be helped from the arena.*

*When a horse runs with speed in the incorrect lead, he's unbalanced and therefore at risk of falling, hurting himself and his rider.*

*Leads are important to a horse's athletic ability. Although they're somewhat complicated, learn to teach them in a way that makes it easy for your horse to understand.*

Here's how to use the Figure-Eight X for lead departures. When circling to the left, stop in the middle of the X. After you stop, cue for a side-pass or leg yield to the left using your right leg. Release the right leg and apply pressure with your left leg and depart into a right-lead canter. Go back to the circle, this time to the right. Come around to the center and stop again in the middle of the X. Since you've been circling right, side-pass or leg yield to the right using your left leg and rein. While side-passing to the right, release your left leg, and immediately apply pressure with your right leg and push to depart into a left lead.

For drop-to-trot lead changes, use the long straightaway of the X. This pattern gives you plenty of time to prepare your horse for the lead changes.

Also, for flying lead changes, the long X is perfect to introduce and position your horse for this advanced maneuver.

## Countercanter

In a countercanter, you change directions, but not leads. For example, if you're circling to the right on a right lead and want to circle to the left, instead of changing leads when you change directions, continue cantering on a right lead in a left circle. This helps prevent your horse from speeding up and anticipating lead changes.

To complete the exercise, go back to the right circle on the right lead. Be sure to work both directions. Countercantering helps develop your horse's strength in the circles and a willingness to change leads on command.

# Figure-Eight X Exercise

 = Side-pass

A. Circle to the left on a left lead.
B. Stop in the middle of the two circles.
C. Side-pass to left, using right-leg pressure. Release right leg and apply left-leg pressure.
D. Depart into right lead in a right circle.
E. Stop in middle of the two circles.
F. Side-pass to the right with left-leg pressure. Release left leg and apply right-leg pressure.
G. Depart into left lead in a left circle.

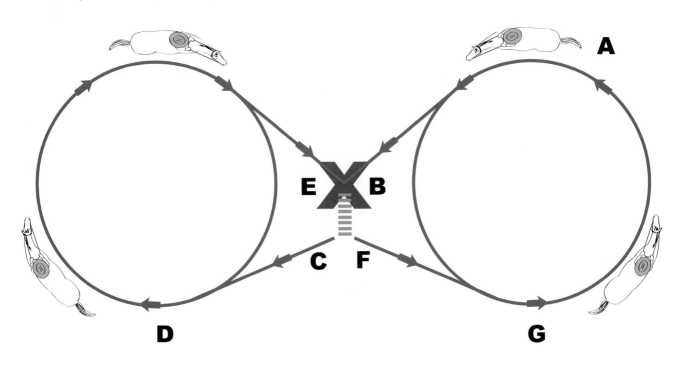

# 18
# THE STOP AND BACK-UP

A great-stopping horse is soft and supple, not only physically, but also mentally. Physically he's relaxed and mentally he understands.

Developing a nice stop on your horse shouldn't be hard. The main thing is preparation. You want him to understand the stop and put effort into slowing down. You don't want him working through fear.

Many people make the mistake of trying to snatch or jerk their horses into the ground. That's a terrible fault because now the horse works through pain, which creates fear. Remember that a bit works through pressure. If you pull hard enough, it works through pain. If your horse is in pain, he can't concentrate on the task at hand. He only anticipates the snatch or jerk, which makes for an out-of-position, nervous and unpredictable horse.

When a horse stops correctly, he puts his weight on his hindquarters and elevates his front end. The main reason a horse stops incorrectly, in other words, on his front end, is that he wasn't prepared. He was out of position at the time he was asked to stop — his head was too high or too low, his body was crooked, or the rider jerked his bit. No one told him he was going to stop. There was no preparation.

Here's how to teach your horse to stop willingly and well.

## Develop the Stop

Start at a walk. The best cues for a stop are to sit down and melt into the saddle, basically stop riding or moving. This

*The best stops are accomplished on a loose rein.*
*A simple "whoa" is all you should need.*

**185**

Quit riding, melt down in the saddle and say "whoa" for a soft stop.

If your horse doesn't stop on command, pick up the reins and hold. The moment he stops, release.

prepares your horse for the stop by signaling to him what you're doing. He feels the change — your lack of movement — so he stops moving, too. At the same time, use one of your most important verbal cues, "whoa." If the horse doesn't respond, only then pick up on the reins and hold. The moment he stops, release your hold.

To walk out again, liven the activity in your seat and allow your horse to follow the feel. Smooch or cluck if he doesn't move; then squeeze with your legs if he still doesn't walk.

Next, move up to a trot and repeat the above. To stop, simply melt down in your saddle and quit riding. Say "whoa." Do this over and over until your horse understands the cues.

One good exercise is getting your horse to "think" stop. Assume a working trot, either through the cones or out on a trail, ask your horse to stop every so often, maybe 10, 12, 15 times. Trot 10 yards, then stop. Trot another 15 yards, stop. Trot 5 yards, stop. Trot 20 yards, stop. What you'll find is that, all of a sudden, your horse anticipates or "thinks" stop. You won't believe how fast he'll pick up on this. I guarantee it. Every time you sit and say "whoa," your horse will think stop and put on the brakes.

Be careful of where your hands are, especially on a young horse. Don't put them too high or low; hold them in a natural way. Be soft and create good habits from the beginning.

## One-Rein Stopping

Don't always use both reins to stop. There are variations of the one-rein stop you can practice to help sharpen your horse. Stopping with one rein keeps your horse softer and more supple because if you constantly pull with both reins, your horse might eventually learn to stiffen and brace against you. If you snatch or jerk, he'll tense his lower jaw or poll, which makes him stiff all over.

Ask for a right-rein stop with a light hold, but support or brace just enough with

*For a one-rein stop, pick up one rein and hold. The next time, use the opposite rein to keep your horse soft and supple.*

*Try placing your hands at an angle. Put one hand down and low and the other hand up and a little higher. This gives your horse a different feel.*

the left rein to keep your horse straight. Next, stop with the left rein and support enough with the right rein to enforce straightness.

Try putting your hands at an angle. For example, for stopping with the right rein, hold your right hand down low and your left hand up a little higher. Stop with the right, support with the left. This is a very effective way to stop and gives your horse a different feel.

Then, reverse the procedure. Drop your left hand down low, support slightly with the right. Next, use both reins to stop your horse. By using a combination of ways to stop, you teach him to give to pressure from either rein in any form. It'll keep your horse light and paying attention to you. Bear in mind, the goal is to achieve a soft or loose-rein stop.

So, in the stop, the most important things are to sit, melt down, say "whoa" and use your hands in a variety of ways.

Take hold of your horse only as much as he needs. In other words, take only as much slack out of the reins as required to stop your horse. Never jerk from a loose rein. If you have to take a good hold of your horse, take the slack out of the reins first, then use those reins as much or little as your horse tells you is necessary. As always, learn to listen to your horse. If your horse wants to pull against you, then hold as much as he pulls. If he's soft, then you be soft. The quicker you release, the lighter your horse will get.

Remember, though, that a good stop comes from straightness. A horse really can't stop well if he's crooked or sideways. The way you get him straight is through the simple flexibility exercises in Chapter 15.

Quality stops aren't about jerking, snatching or rushing the horse. It's the preparation from the rider that allows the horse to follow a feel. Good stops are about teaching and not making the horse stop. Build in the "want-to."

## Stopping Through Inspiration or Desperation

Good stops come from understanding, patience and consistency. There are many factors that go into the big stop — fencing techniques, sliding plates (horseshoes), good ground, good breeding and conformation all contribute. However, nothing is more important than good fundamentals taught slowly and individually with each horse.

The most common mistake you can make in teaching your horse to stop is the use of force. When a horse doesn't stop, the typical fix is to get a bigger bit. As you jerk, snatch, pull and haul on the reins, the horse only gets worse. The harder you pull, the higher the horse's head goes and the faster

## HERE'S HOW

### Stop and Back

If your horse has a tendency to walk forward out of the stop, doesn't really use his hindquarters, or braces at the stop, here's what to do.

Ask for the stop, give a quick release on the reins as a reward, but then back your horse immediately. Say "whoa" as you back.

It should happen like this: Stop the horse, say "whoa," release the reins, then back him saying "whoa, whoa, whoa."

Release again and drive your horse forward.

Go 10 yards and stop.

Say "whoa." Release, back him again.

Another version: Ask for a stop and keep your hold on the reins. Don't release as above. Maintain your hold on the reins, saying "whoa" until your horse takes a step backward. When he does, then release your hold. Now, your horse will really think stop and get on his hindquarters because when he does, you'll release him.

You also can use a combination of rein bumps as you hold: right rein, left rein, right rein, left rein to back.

Then, don't forget to release.

*For the horse, incentives for a good stop are release, relief and reward.*

he runs. The horse runs away from the pressure and pain you create.

The best stops, like all other maneuvers, are achieved by the incentives of release, relief and reward. When a horse finds softness in a stop, then he wants to do it. A horse with want-to is capable of greatness. Most horses I've seen that ran off or wouldn't stop were either very green or somewhat abused. The running off came from fear. When there's fear, there's an instinctive response. The horse's strongest instinct in time of trouble is to run. When a horse runs because he's afraid, he thinks he's running for his life and this can be extremely dangerous. A horse at this stage of panic could very well kill himself and, if you're on his back, he might take you with him.

To avoid this frightening scenario, use good common sense, which I call horse sense. Listen to your horse and develop good horsemanship fundamentals. Keep in mind, teaching is the art of communication and communication is two minds listening — yours and your horse's.

## The Back-Up

Backing isn't natural to the horse. It's not something he'd normally do out on the range or in a pasture. It's a maneuver you have to teach your horse.

Having a good back-up shows you have a lot of control over your horse. In backing, a horse really has to use his hindquarters, and that's where all great performance takes place. So it's a maneuver worth developing well.

## A Two-Beat Gait

The back-up is a diagonal, two-beat gait, like the trot, but backward. As your horse backs, when he picks up the right front foot, he also picks up the left rear. And, when he picks up the left front foot, he picks up the right rear at the same time.

**189**

*For a correct back, the horse should give at the poll, which elevates the shoulders and places more weight on the hindquarters. Note the horse moving in a two-beat gait — right front and left rear legs are moving simultaneously.*

Any other pattern to his footfalls isn't a true or correct back. When you see a horse dragging his feet back in any other sequence, he's resisting the back-up and not performing it properly.

## Developing a Good Back-Up

Develop the back-up one step at a time. The mistake most people make is that they want to pull a horse backward. Don't pull, guide!

What's the horse looking for in almost everything we do with him? It's the release from pressure. It's the relief, reward and relaxation he gets from following cues correctly that's the horse's incentive to perform.

The correct position for the horse to back is to round his spine, to collect. As I've explained before, almost every mammal has seven vertebrae in his neck. The first two nearest the head are the atlas and axis; that's where you want your horse to give. For the horse, this is his poll area and you want him to give or "break" at the poll. When he does that, it elevates his shoulders and back and places more weight on his hindquarters, which makes it easier for the horse to back.

If you pull or tug your horse back, his head will come up, his shoulders will go down and that puts more weight on the front end. Now it's tougher for the horse to back.

When you teach your horse to back, exaggerate your cues at first. Hold the reins with slight pressure, say "back" and when you see your horse picking up his right front foot, pick up your right rein. The next foot to move is the left front. Pick up your left rein as the left front leaves the ground. This is all part of your timing. You can get in rhythm with his feet — right, left, right, left.

Again, work one rein at a time and use your legs, as well. Use your feet in

**Rein-leg Timing**

*1. See which leg your horse is about to pick up. Here, the left front is about to come off the ground. This is when you want to pick up the left rein.*

*2. Hold slight pressure on the left rein as the horse picks up his left front foot and puts it down. Next, you'll pick up the right rein as the right front foot comes off the ground.*

cadence with your hands. For example, when the horse's right front foot comes off the ground, lift your right rein and bump your right foot on his right shoulder. With practice, the timing of your cues will be in rhythm with your horse's feet.

## Guiding Backward

You can guide your horse straight back or to the right or left. The easiest way to straighten a crooked back is to position your horse's shoulders in the same direction. In other words, if you want to back straight and your horse's hindquarters drift to the left, move his

## A BETTER WAY

### Let Gravity Help

For a horse that's having trouble understanding or one that's learned to brace against you when you ask for a back-up, ride him up a small hill or incline, say, to the edge of a tank dam, and let gravity help. Hold with gentle pressure on the reins and wait for your horse to step backward. Then immediately release your hold.

As you hold with your reins, use slight bumps with your legs on his sides or even up on his shoulders. As before, the second he moves back, release your hold. And don't forget your verbal cue, "back."

This is an easy way to encourage your horse to do the right thing. Work through holding, guiding or releasing, not jerking, hauling or forcing.

**191**

shoulders to the left and that'll straighten him out. If he veers his hindquarters to the right, move his shoulders to the right and he'll line out.

The flexibility exercises help you to achieve straightness. Remember, straightness is crucial to good horsemanship. And, amazingly, the way you get straightness is through flexibility. You'll find that every one of these basics feeds right into another one. One is an extension of the other. You won't get one without the other. What's a stop? It's an extension of the gallop. What is a back-up? It's an extension of the stop. Good basic fundamentals, as always, are the key.

***One mistake to avoid:*** Don't back your horse until he quits you. If you feel your horse getting nervous, tight, or tense and maybe a little sticky with his legs, or his head comes up, quit before the horse quits. Make it your idea to quit, not his.

To get your horse ready to back again, drive him forward. Loosen him up. Maybe even circle the cones. Stop and ask him to back again.

If you back your horse till he quits, what did you teach the horse? You've taught him to quit. So stop asking for a back before you feel your horse wanting to quit. That's all part of learning to read and outthink your horse.

When you can back a complete circle, you'll have complete control over your horse's body from his head, neck, shoulders and rib cage through his hindquarters.

## Weaving Backward Through the Cones

Weaving backward through the cones is a good exercise to sharpen your horse's back-up. The hindquarters-control exercise mentioned in Chapter 15, where you walk the horse's back end around his front end, comes in handy here. With control over your horse's hindquarters, you can actually guide your horse with your legs, and position his head, neck and shoulders to weave through the cones backward.

Start on the outside of the circle with the cones to your left. Actually turn around and look where you're going.

First, engage your horse backward. Pick up the reins and establish control. If you want to move your horse's hindquarters to turn to the left between the cones, pick up your right rein and move your horse's head, neck and shoulders to the right, at the same time using your right leg to push the hindquarters to the left, through the cones.

# A BETTER WAY

## Running Away

Horses that run off usually have panicked and reverted to the strong self-preservation instinct. These horses usually have big engines and, on that particular day, they have a little too much energy.

Before you ride out the gate on a high-powered horse, take him to a round pen or corral and warm him up. Make him circle at liberty 20 to 25 times each direction, whatever it takes. Offer a resting spot near you when he relaxes and turns loose. You'll know when that happens because the horse drops his head, works his ears and licks his lips.

If you find yourself in a runaway situation, don't try to stop your horse with two reins. Your horse could brace against them.

Bend your horse with a one-rein stop. It might take all your strength, but bend him until you can turn him; and if you can turn him, you can stop him.

If you feel your horse is becoming unbalanced with your pull, ease up, then bend again. The same thing goes for a horse that doesn't immediately respond to the one-rein stop. Have the presence of mind to release him, then pick up the rein and bend again. Keep it up. It's like reconnecting a circuit. Horses get into a panic mode, and you have to rewire them to get through to the brain.

A horse that regularly runs off probably wasn't really broke to begin with. Go back to all the basics and restart your horse.

Use a left and right rein action in rhythm with your horse's feet to keep your horse stepping back.

Now, your horse needs to turn his hindquarters right between the next cones. Pick up your left rein and move his head, neck and shoulders to the left, which automatically shifts his hindquarters to the right. Release your right leg and use your left leg to help push his hindquarters over to the right.

This is all a give-and-take motion, where you find a rhythm. If, at any time, you feel your horse get the least bit sticky, release and drive him forward. Then, start again.

In the beginning, you might not get all the way around the cones, but just begin somewhere. Before you know it, you'll have a really fluid back.

Sometimes backing requires a little bit of a waiting game, especially in the beginning. Allow your horse to follow a feel. When you get one step back, make sure you release. Build off that one step. Notice when your horse tries and reward that try. It's not the pull, but the release the horse looks for. Pretty soon, it's two steps, three steps and then more. A horse that backs well can back almost as fast as he can trot, because it's the same gait, but backward.

*To move your horse's hindquarters to the right backward, pick up on the left rein and turn your horse's head, neck and shoulders to the left. That automatically moves the horse's hindquarters to the right.*

## True Story: A Dead Run

A runaway horse is a dangerous horse, to himself and his rider. The result can sometimes be injury or death.

Years ago, I was part of the crew working cattle on a south Texas ranch. It was a hot day and all the livestock, cattle and horses, were on edge. A heavy-handed cowboy, who'd been somewhat abusive to his horse by continually jerking and pulling on the reins without any slack, reaped what he sowed. When he took off after a stray cow, the horse just quit him. In a blind panic and at a dead run, the horse headed into heavy brush and timber. With all his strength, the cowboy pulled on both reins to no avail. As the pair entered the brush, a thick, low branch off a big oak tree caught "ol' heavy hands" dead-center and

chest-high and just ripped him backward off his horse. He landed with a heavy thud, and the rest of us thought surely he must be dead.

He wasn't, and later we all had a good laugh. But actually, this incident could've ended in disaster.

It's often said that the horse seeks the level of his rider. In this case, the only way the horse found any release was to run away and get rid of the source of his pain.

A bigger bit won't make your horse stop better; understanding will. Horsemanship is like life; you get what you give. If you give it rough and tough, there's a good chance you'll receive it rough and tough. If you give it with meaning and purpose, it'll return to you in kind.

*"To ride without proper hindquarter engagement and control is like dancing without music."*

# 19

# WORK OFF THE HINDQUARTERS — PIVOTS, ROLLBACKS AND SPINS

Nothing is more beautiful to watch than great athletes in action. For example, seeing a great reining horse stop or spin, an outstanding cow horse hold an intimidating cow with confidence and determination or a Grand Pix dressage horse make lead changes every stride is thrilling for all horse enthusiasts. Achieving such perfection at that level takes talent on the part of the horse and the rider.

Two things all great performance horses have in common are athletic ability and quality training. These horses have been taught to use their hindquarters effectively, and outstanding hindquarter maneuvers translate into balance and beauty.

One thing I've come to realize is that superior horsemanship, be it cutting, reining, barrel racing, jumping, dressage or any discipline, is a result of solid fundamentals. Teaching a horse to work off his hindquarters with position and balance is paramount and one of the keys to high-level performance.

*A horse's engine is in his hindquarters and their control is critical to high-performance maneuvers.*

The hair stands up on my neck when I watch Al Dunning perform a 40-foot slide on a top reined cow horse. Witnessing Buster Welch riding a great cutting horse that practically sits down on his hindquarters to look like a predator while working cattle is breathtaking. These horses know how to use their hindquarters, and you can tell they love it. A balanced horse performs better. To control the hindquarters is to control the engine of the horse.

To ride without proper hindquarter engagement and control is like dancing without music. It's just not as good.

This chapter offers exercises designed to develop and improve hindquarter maneuvers.

## Doubling Exercise

A simple change of direction or doubling into a fence is where you begin to really put the "handle" (rein-ability) on your horse. It teaches your horse to further follow a feel. This exercise, like many of the others, is done with one rein at a time and typically with a snaffle bit. If you've done your homework with a snaffle bit, you can develop just about any high-level maneuver.

Follow along the fence, with it on your right side. Don't get too close because your horse will run into it when you turn toward it or it'll stop him altogether. And, if it's a low fence, he might even put his head over it. But don't be too far away either, or using the fence for this exercise won't be as effective.

Ride approximately 3 feet away so that when you turn your horse, the fence acts as a barrier and pushes him to turn on his hindquarters.

This is a moving turn. You don't stop the horse or perform a reining-type rollback, which is a full stop, followed by a turn in the opposite direction. However, it comes close and is the precursor for such performance moves.

If you're more comfortable starting at a walk, you could, but a trot is better and easier for your horse

because of the increased momentum. Eventually, you should be able to perform this exercise at a canter or lope. By this time, you should be good at handling your reins and direct-reining your horse.

In direct-reining during this exercise, bend your horse to the right toward the fence with your right rein. Don't snatch or jerk your horse around. Instead, take the slack out of the rein with more of a steady pull toward your right hip.

If your horse can't follow that suggestion, lead out with your right hand as you've done in previous exercises. Let him follow that, then come back toward your hip.

Done correctly, this exercise loosens up your horse's front end, especially his shoulders. Your horse doesn't move his front feet forward, he reaches out to the side. He leads with his nose, moves his front end across and pivots on his hindquarters. This is the beginning of a real performance-horse maneuver. Examples: In a reining rollback, a horse reaches out and crosses over with his front feet. In a reining spin or turnaround, the horse reaches out with one foot and crosses over with the other. In a leg-yield or two-track, the horse reaches out with one foot and crosses over with the other. These are performance horse moves and this is where it all begins. Loosening up his front end teaches your horse to work off of his hindquarters.

In making a 180-degree turn to the right, the important part is the release. Don't pull your horse through the turn; guide him through it. Ideally, at about 90 degrees, he's already made the turn, so release your right rein.

As you release, apply pressure with your supporting leg and rein to follow through the turn. Your supporting leg is your outside or left leg (press the horse's left rib cage) and your supporting rein is your outside or left rein (lay or push it on your horse's neck). Ride your horse off. It's the riding off that gets your horse good at this exercise. He learns to use himself through a turn, and he doesn't look for a place to stop. He loosens or picks up his front end and pushes off with his hindquarters — that's what this exercise is all about.

## Protective Gear

Use the right equipment for performance work. Put splint or protective boots on your horse's legs to protect them. Otherwise, your horse could accidentally injure himself. If the maneuver hurts, he might not want to perform it again.

It's important here that you don't spur your horse or use your outside leg too quickly. If you spur your horse before you direct with your reins, he could go the wrong direction.

As for yourself, don't just sit there, rise up slightly out of your saddle and help your horse get up out of the ground and move through the turn.

Ride another 30 yards or so and change directions again. Use the reverse cues to turn to the left on a fence. Bend your horse into the fence with your left rein. Once he's committed to the turn about 90 degrees, release your left rein, lay your right rein on the right side of your horse's neck and add right leg pressure to ride your horse through the turn.

Vary the length between turns — go 40 yards next time, then 20 yards, then 30. Keep it varied and interesting for your horse. Keep him guessing as to where he'll turn. He'll soon become real light in your hands and handy in his turns. You're starting to put a handle on your horse. What's he chasing or looking for? The release. That's what

1. Ride with the fence or rail on your right, approximately 3 feet away. To double to the right, use your right rein and turn horse into the fence.

2. As soon as the horse passes the 90-degree mark, release the right rein.

3. Ride out of the turn and continue down the fence, with it now on your left.

1. About midway down the fence, Craig turns or doubles the horse into the fence with the left rein.

2. Note how this horse uses his hindquarters to stabilize himself through the turn.

3. The horse then pushes off with power in his hindquarters to complete the turn and move off.

makes the horse great. If you're consistent in your timing of the release, I promise you your horse will get lighter and lighter and lighter.

If you're inconsistent and the release comes at odd times, your horse could get heavier and heavier.

## Rear-End Pivot

A rear-end pivot is a turn on the haunches or hindquarters and is a refinement of doubling.

The zigzag, pivot-foot and wagon-wheel exercises I describe here help develop your horse's rear-end pivot, as well as the back-up, stop, spin and rollback.

## Zigzag Exercise

The zigzag exercise gives you a way to accomplish the rear-end pivot by making it easy and logical for your horse to do so.

Set up your cones in a pattern where you ride in a zigzag fashion. Place them approximately 20 yards from one another. Set up a series of 10 cones (two at each pivot point) that form gates you ride and back through. (See Zigzag exercise diagram.)

The objective is to ride your horse through them, stop between them, back, then turn in the other direction. You can do this at a walk, trot or canter, but it's best to have some speed. A trot and canter are the most practical gaits for this exercise.

The back-up is important here, just like in the back-up exercises. Whether you're on the side of a hill or backing through the cones or backing in circles, it teaches your horse to use his hindquarters and literally puts him on his hindquarters. Just as before, your horse should be in the correct position to back. He should break at the poll, his shoulders should be elevated, his front feet loosened up to move and the majority of his weight should be on his hindquarters.

In a zigzag, ride your horse to one set of cones, stop, back, then turn to the left and ride to the next set of cones. Stop, back, then turn to the right and ride down to the next set of cones. Make the turn while your horse is backing.

Don't back, stop, then turn. Your horse might start to walk forward if you do and that won't be a true rear-end pivot. The back-up and turn are one continuous movement.

The whole idea for the zigzag is to drive forward, stop, back, and while your horse is backing, turn in the other direction. It's a change of direction and anywhere from a 45- to 180-degree turn. But you also can back and pivot in a 360-degree turn and ride off or a 90-degree turn and ride off. Vary it however you like and in time your horse will become very handy and light in your hands.

Your hands and legs also help out in this maneuver. Look in the direction you're turning; don't look down at your horse, watch where you're going.

For example, in a pivot to the right: Look to the right, open up your right rein, take your right leg off your horse's side, and apply pressure with your left rein and leg, helping to push your horse through the turn.

Lead your horse in the direction you want to go while he's backing. That's what keeps him on his hindquarters.

## Zigzag Exercise

▶▶▶▶▶▶ = Back-up

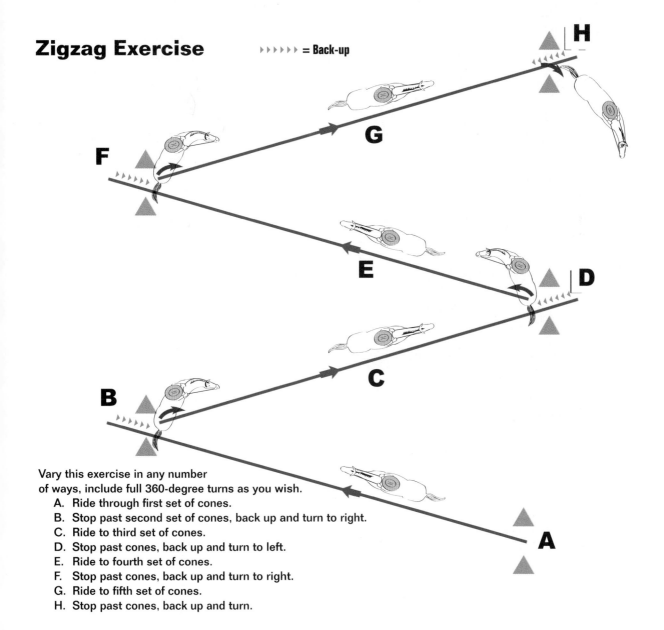

Vary this exercise in any number
of ways, include full 360-degree turns as you wish.
   A.  Ride through first set of cones.
   B.  Stop past second set of cones, back up and turn to right.
   C.  Ride to third set of cones.
   D.  Stop past cones, back up and turn to left.
   E.  Ride to fourth set of cones.
   F.  Stop past cones, back up and turn to right.
   G.  Ride to fifth set of cones.
   H.  Stop past cones, back up and turn.

*1. Ride from one cone to the next and stop.*

*2. Back a few steps.*

*3. As you're backing, turn your horse to the right (or left) and continue to the next cone.*

## Pivot-Foot Exercise

The pivot-foot exercise develops the stationary pivot foot, which is important to the rollback and turnaround.

Ride forward into a tight circle to the right, stop and immediately pivot or spin to the left. (See Pivot-Foot Exercise diagram.) After you pivot, stop, ride forward into a tight circle or spin to the left. Stop and immediately pivot to the right. Ride a few more strides, make a tight circle or spin to the right, stop, then roll back or spin the opposite direction and move forward again. This teaches a horse a lot about following a feel, stopping on his hindquarters, then rolling out or spinning with a good rear-end pivot foot.

## Wagon-Wheel Exercise

I call this exercise "wagon wheel" because you work from the center of the cones outward like the spokes of a wheel. (See Wagon-Wheel

## Pivot Foot Exercise

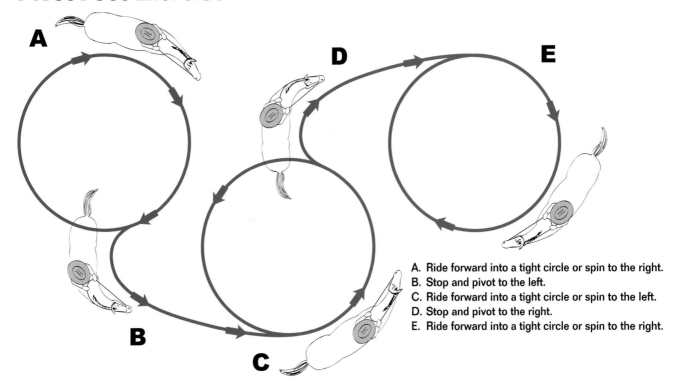

A. Ride forward into a tight circle or spin to the right.
B. Stop and pivot to the left.
C. Ride forward into a tight circle or spin to the left.
D. Stop and pivot to the right.
E. Ride forward into a tight circle or spin to the right.

## Wagon-Wheel Exercise

You can vary this pattern by pivoting 90, 180 or even 360 degrees.

A. Start at the center or hub of a 40-foot circle and ride to one of the cones.
B. Stop and back all the way to hub.
C. Pivot 90 degrees.
D. Ride to next cone.
E. Stop and back all the way to hub.
F. Pivot 180 degrees.
G. Ride to next cone.

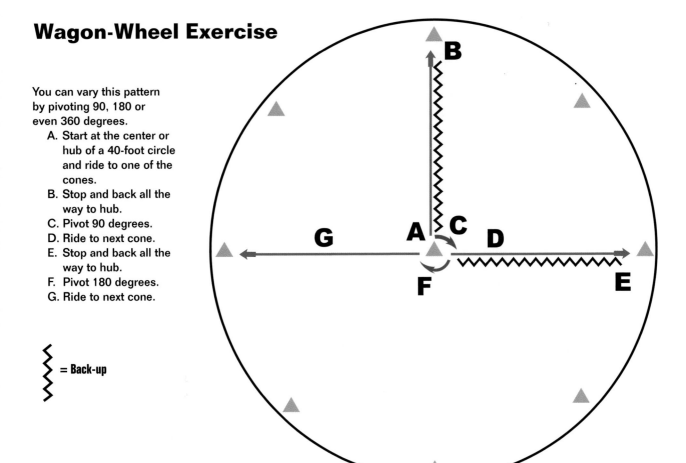

= Back-up

exercise diagram.) You also can work from the center of any circle or even the center of a round pen. In other words, you need a center point. For the sake of explanation, though, I'll assume you're working with cones.

Drive your horse to the rim of the wagon wheel or edge of the cones. You can do so at any gait — walk, trot, canter — as long as you're in control. Stop and back your horse all the way to the hub or center point. Place the cones so the hub or middle is approximately 20 feet from the cones or perimeter. You want it big enough for working room, but not so big you have to back too far.

*Remember:* In order for your horse to really back well, you must turn loose of him so his feet can move. If you over-bend him with one rein or the other, the hindquarters move too much. Straightness in the horse while backing is key.

When you reach the hub, pivot, just as you did in the zigzag exercise. Pivot as much as you want — a 90-degree turn, 180 or even 360. Then drive your horse to the rim of the circle in the new direction you now face. Then, back to the hub again. Repeat this exercise over and over and notice how effortlessly your horse starts to drive forward, stop, back, turn and then push off his hindquarters to develop a rear-end pivot.

You might try working one direction at a time. For example, when you back to the hub, perform every pivot, rollback or spin to the left. You'll find your horse really starts anticipating left-hand turns, and that helps him develop himself in that direction. Once you've done this numerous times, try spinning your horse at the hub several 360 revolutions. Find a good stopping spot and let your horse rest.

# A BETTER WAY

## Back into the Rollback

A good way to teach your horse to pivot off his hindquarters or if he's sticky in his stops is to use the back-up to teach him the rollback. Hold a rein in each hand, ask your horse to back a few steps and as he's backing, turn him, say to the right, with your right rein. The moment he initiates the turn, release and ride off. Stop again, back a few steps and as he's backing, turn to the left with your left rein. Release when he turns. Ride off.

Next, do nothing but right-hand turns. Once you feel your horse is fairly handy at this exercise, shorten it. In the center or hub, just move a step or two forward, then stop, back and pivot. Now, instead of moving to the edge of the wagon wheel, revolve around the hub in short, little pivots.

After a job well done, stop and let your horse rest and breathe. Remember the stopping spots in any exercise. That's when you give it all back to the horse. It's the release he's looking for. He'll know and understand that. This is where a horse learns to really become gentle and well-broke.

# Rollback

These exercises take you right into the rollback. It's amazing how all of them work together. They build upon one another.

A true rollback is a 180-degree turn on the hindquarters. The difference between a rollback and doubling is that you actually come to a stop in the rollback before you make the turn.

Since you've already practiced stopping and doubling, your horse should be ready for this high-performance maneuver.

Position yourself alongside the fence as before in the doubling exercise. Start at the trot, if you wish, to stay under control in the beginning. You can always work up to the canter or lope.

As you trot along the fence, ask for a stop, sit down in the saddle and say "whoa." The second your horse has stopped, but before he stands up again, turn him into the fence with one rein.

Don't pull your horse backward into the turn. However, if your horse doesn't work properly off his hindquarters and gets sticky in his stops, you might have to back him a step or two to help him get back on his hocks. Then turn him. Some horses are more natural and some are just a little slower than others at learning to use their hindquarters. (See "A Better Way" titled "Back into the Rollback.")

When a horse stops correctly, he's naturally down on his hindquarters. Use one

1. Stop alongside the fence, leaving enough room to turn into it. Note, this horse has stopped properly on his hindquarters.

2. Use your right rein to turn the horse into the fence. The crouch in the horse's hindquarters is still evident.

3. The horse should bring his front end across, powering off his hindquarters.

*4. As soon as you turn, release the right rein and lope off. The horse's hindquarters are pushing him off into the canter.*

rein, say, the right rein if you're moving down the fence on your right. Your horse should make a natural pivot to the right. You want your horse to be soft and supple in his front end and that's what you accomplish by using one rein.

Just as in doubling, after you release your right rein, for example at 90 degrees, use outside or left leg pressure and lay your left rein against the left side of your horse's neck. Again, rise slightly out of your saddle to help your horse and ride him out of the turn. This is what will make him handy in his rollbacks, just as in doubling.

Practice going down the fence in both directions. Offer your horse a loose-rein stop.

Sit down and say "whoa." If he doesn't stop, use your combination of reins to stop him. For example, in a left rollback, use more of your left rein to stop. The combination would be to stop him with the left rein and brace with the right rein. By stopping more with the left rein, your horse is naturally prepared to go to the left. Once he stops, then roll him back with just the left rein and go.

Prepare for every move you do. Just like my friends Ray Hunt and the late Tom Dorrance have always said: "Prepare and position for everything you do."

As many times as you practice the rollback, your horse might anticipate the turn and turn before you ask him to. If he does, just stop, walk forward or maybe make a small circle in the opposite direction. Keep him waiting on you. The reason? You want to be the leader and the horse the follower.

# 360-degree Spin or Turnaround

The next most logical progression from a rollback is a complete 360-degree turnaround. The spin or turnaround is a reining-horse performance maneuver that really shows the horse's athleticism and the control the rider has over the horse. It's gorgeous when done correctly. You can easily accomplish the basics of this maneuver with the doubling and rollback exercises.

Understand the mechanics of the spin, which is mostly forward movement. Many riders make the mistake of trying to pull their horses back into this spin. A horse can't turn around if you pull him backward.

I like to develop a spin through a lot of one-rein work. There are several ways to accomplish the turnaround. One is through the rollback exercise. Do your rollback work and then add on.

Go down the fence, say to the right, stop your horse, roll back, but roll all the way into a 360-degree turn. This time, instead of making a 180-degree turn, you've made a complete 360-degree turn. You should face the same direction you were going.

You can go farther with this and make a turn and a half — first a 180-degree turn or rollback, followed by a complete 360-degree turn, which puts you facing the opposite direction you started. Someday, you'll be able to hold your horse into several turns. In the beginning, make sure you ride him out of the spins when you're through, instead of stopping. That way he thinks about spinning and not stopping. Your horse needs to use his hindquarters to pivot and push his front legs into the turn. His front legs should reach out and cross over. Understand that spinning is about controlled forward movement, and when it's done correctly it's a stationary turn that's flat and fast.

*In a correct 360-degree turnaround, the horse's front legs reach out and cross over.*

# Small-Circle Spin

Another way to work on the spin is to walk small forward-movement circles. The key word here is forward movement. Walk forward, forward, forward. If you make the circle small enough with forward movement and supple your horse while doing it, you'll be amazed at what this will do.

For example, walk forward-movement circles to the left. Push with your seat bones and drive your horse forward. Look down at the ground to your left and find a center or focal point, like a rock, so you know you're staying in the same spot. Using your left rein, tip your horse's nose slightly to the left and look for his right front foot to step across his left front foot. If you make this circle small enough, the horse's front end

# HERE'S HOW

## Combinations

All the exercises I've offered in this book are good for any age horse, but this is a particularly good one that combines all of them. It includes the circle, stop, back-up, roll back and lead change.

For this exercise, you'll use the cones, placed in the same four-cornered pattern you've worked these exercises in, and a nearby fence. The fence helps with straightness in the stop and rollback and the cones help to maintain a nice, round circle.

Start by riding off in a circle. You can work at a walk, trot or canter. Ideally, in the end you perform these combinations in a canter, but start with the speed that you're most comfortable with.

From the circle, ride toward the fence at about a 45-degree angle, allowing the fence to help you stop. As you do, don't forget to say "whoa" and melt down in the saddle.

From the stop, roll back in the opposite direction. Back a few steps if necessary to achieve a smooth roll back. Ideally, come out in a canter, having changed leads, and return to the circle in the opposite direction.

You can vary this combination exercise by not stopping every time. Just keep circling to prevent your horse from anticipating the stop and change of direction.

## Combinations Exercise

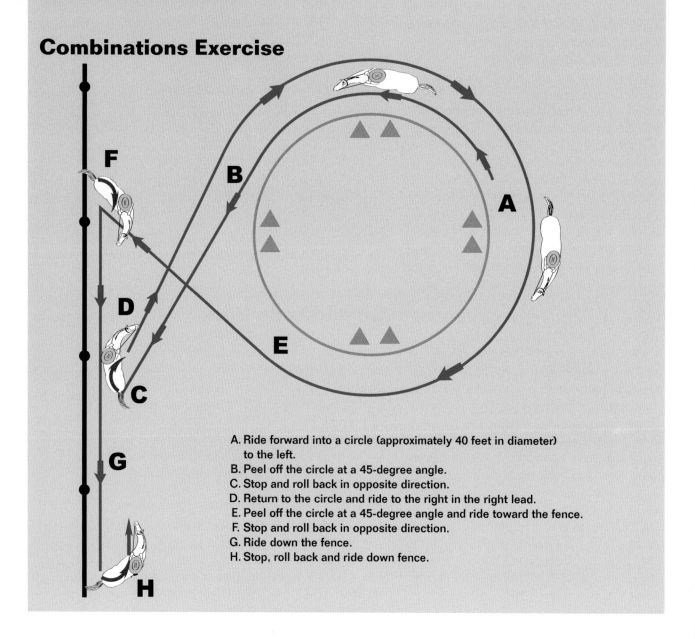

A. Ride forward into a circle (approximately 40 feet in diameter) to the left.
B. Peel off the circle at a 45-degree angle.
C. Stop and roll back in opposite direction.
D. Return to the circle and ride to the right in the right lead.
E. Peel off the circle at a 45-degree angle and ride toward the fence.
F. Stop and roll back in opposite direction.
G. Ride down the fence.
H. Stop, roll back and ride down fence.

travels a greater distance than his hind end. You'll feel your horse reach out and across with his front legs, and when you do he's ready to pivot or turn around.

At this point, engage your outside or right leg on his right rib cage and outside or right rein on the right side of his neck and simply try to move your horse's front end around the hind end. Make it easy for your horse to turn around. In the beginning, you might get just a quarter-pivot or half-pivot, but that's okay. Ride your horse out of the turn and go right back to the same circle.

In the beginning, work one direction at a time to get your horse really working with you. Make many small circles, pushing with your seat bones and driving your horse forward, then pivot and drive him back to the circle. This is very important: Do it over and over until your horse learns how to place his feet before you ever expect him to perform it with speed. It's a mistake to try to get your horse to spin fast before he learns how to place his feet.

If you have a horse that has a tendency to walk out of the circle or not use his hindquarters, at the end of the sequence of walking the small circles, step your horse backward, turn him around and walk him off. Find a corner, say of an arena, and use the 90-degree angle to do the circles in. That helps the horse to stay focused and centered. You can drive him into the corner repeatedly and then begin to turn him around with your outside leg and outside rein. As you turn, say to the left, really open up with the left rein to help your horse. Let him bend and turn into the spin.

One of the common mistakes in spinning to the left is pulling too much on the left rein. If you pull too hard or overly bend the horse, his hindquarters move too much and that's not what you want in a spin.

In other words, you don't want the horse to be over-bent, but it's okay for your horse to be slightly bent and naturally looking in the direction he's going. Over-bending in many maneuvers is a common mistake.

The speed comes from your legs, not your reins. Encourage speed by increasing your leg pressure and/or clucking or smooching. The definition of a great spin is flat and fast, as I mentioned above. But in the beginning, make it correct and slow and, in time, you'll accomplish flat and fast.

## True Story: Hammer Time

*At one of the annual Michael Martin Murphey WestFests in Copper Mountain, Colo., I was brought a 10-year-old mustang stallion to work for the demonstration. This horse was notorious for charging and kicking with both back feet.*

*Working in front of a large crowd and knowing I was challenged, I decided the best way to handle this outlaw was to work from another horse. My best horse at that time was a big, stout Quarter Horse gelding named Hammer. This was not Hammer's first tough horse.*

*Although Hammer was big, he was athletic. Through training, Hammer was apt at working off and turning on his hindquarters. When we approached, the unruly stallion charged, as*

*expected. Hammer was too fast for him and made an incredible turn on the hindquarters to avoid the attacker. Whether the mustang kicked, pawed, charged or bit, Hammer was able to evade him with lightning-quick hindquarter pivots and turns.*

*These maneuvers enabled me to eventually get close enough to finally handle the horse. In time, I was able to complete the breaking and gentling process and ride the renegade.*

*Without Hammer's quick hindquarter movements, success wouldn't have been possible. If he'd tried to turn on the forehand, we'd have been too slow to steer clear of the danger.*

*All great performance horses work off their hindquarters. The spin, stop, rollback and most all advanced maneuvers generate from the hindquarters.*

# 20
# TRAILER LOADING

The biggest mistake in trailer loading is that people try to make their horses get into the trailer instead of teaching them to get into the trailer. Trailer loading, like almost everything else I've discussed thus far, is about taking the fear out of the horse. As prey animals, horses don't like to walk into trailers because they're small, dark, closed and confined, like caves, where predators can lurk. As a natural claustrophobic, a prey animal would probably not put himself in that situation in the first place.

Never forget that when you put a horse in a trailer, you take away the single most important thing to him — his ability to run away. So, there's a real trust present when you ask a horse to step into a trailer.

## Prepare Before You Load

First of all, teach trailer loading in a safe trailer. It doesn't matter if it's a two-horse inline or six-horse stock trailer, it needs to have good, solid flooring with thick rubber mats and no harmful protrusions.

Attach the trailer to your hauling vehicle or chock the wheels to make sure it won't move during the loading process. If your trailer doesn't have a loading ramp, park the trailer so that the back end is in a low spot, making it easier for your horse to load and unload during training sessions. This isn't always possible, but it's a good idea.

Open the trailer doors wide. As you introduce the trailer to your horse, you'll go through ground work at the back end of your trailer.

*The horse loads so willingly, Craig flips the lead rope over his back as the horse moves inside.*

The Paint shows the typical resistance of a horse not wanting to load in the trailer.

With a halter and 12-foot lead rope on the horse and a swagger stick, longe the horse in front of the trailer opening.

## Take a Test Ride in Your Trailer

I recommend that you take a ride in your trailer. Have a friend drive your rig and you play the part of the horse. Then, you'll experience trailering from your horse's perspective. You'll understand what your horse goes through when the trailer accelerates, turns and stops. You'll appreciate the balancing act he undergoes just to stand up straight in the trailer. Don't cheat by grabbing onto something. Stand there with your arms at your sides, like a horse has to do. The first thing you'll find yourself doing is spreading out your legs and standing sideways.

The experience makes a better driver out of you. Your stops, starts and turns will be gradual because you know what happens when they're not.

Don't put a time limit on your trailer-loading lesson. A common mistake is to try to load the horse the day you need to go somewhere. Start days or weeks ahead of time and have quiet, no-rush sessions.

The key to trailer loading is having forward movement. (See Chapter 16, "Forward Movement Exercises.") With it, you can get a horse to load in any trailer, anywhere, any time and any place.

Put a rope halter and 12-foot lead rope on your horse and have your swagger stick handy. Longe him by the trailer doors, say, going to the left, several feet away at first. At some point, move closer and closer to the trailer, with forward movement. You want to get your horse's mind on the trailer.

Your philosophy throughout will be: Make the right thing easy and the wrong thing difficult. In other words, loading in the trailer is the right thing and not loading is the wrong thing.

As your horse circles around, allow him to stop at the back end of the trailer and look inside. It piques his curiosity. Just as with any scary object — a tarp, water crossing, log, bridge — let your horse look at it, smell it. When he stops to investigate the trailer, reward him by letting him rest and stand there inspecting the trailer. That's the right thing to do, so make it easy for him. And rub him to reassure him.

When you see your horse's mind drift and he no longer appears interested in the trailer, ask for forward movement again. Put him back to work with more circles. Let his resting spot be at the trailer's door.

## Watch for the "Try"

At some point, ask your horse for a "try," which means forward movement or a step into the trailer. Raise your left hand toward the trailer (assuming your horse is on your right), suggesting he move inside. If he doesn't, tap his hindquarters with the swagger stick. Note, I said "tap," not anything stronger.

When he puts one front foot on the floorboards, consider that a try. Stop tapping. He might jerk his foot back right away, but at least he tried. Look for the positive things your horse gives you. Don't look for what isn't happening, but what is. Notice the slightest changes in his demeanor.

Put your horse to work on more circles until you see him look toward the inside of the trailer again. Allow him to stop and when he does encourage him to step into the trailer. This time he might put two feet inside.

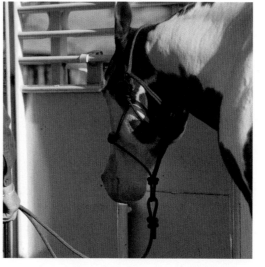

*When he shows interest in the trailer, allow the horse to stop and catch his breath at the trailer door. There, he can rest as he looks inside.*

This is where a lot of people make a tremendous mistake. They start whipping or trying to make the horse go the rest of the way in.

One of the most important things you can teach your horse in trailer loading is that he can get out as well as get in. He needs to know that he's not trapped in there.

When he has two feet in, he'll probably want to back out quickly. Let him. It's okay. Don't become frustrated.

Ask him to load again. If he doesn't want to or starts to back or pull on you,

*This horse is exhibiting a "try" and lifing his foot onto the trailer floorboard. The "go past" cue or tap on the hindquarters encourages forward movement into the trailer.*

*If necessary, stand in the trailer to reassure your horse that everything is okay.*

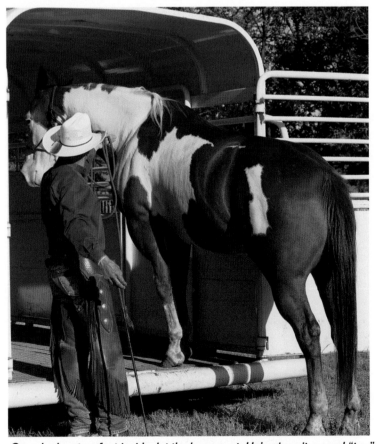

*Once he has two feet inside, let the horse rest. He's given it a good "try."*

put him to work with more circles. Wrong thing, work; right thing, relief. And, as before, the only resting spot is in front of the trailer door.

When he puts two of his front feet inside again, rub him to build trust and confidence.

## Go-Past Cue

For a horse that's reluctant to get all the way into the trailer at this point, go back to a forward-movement exercise outside the trailer or even in the round pen. In this exercise, though, your objective is for your horse to move past you as you tap him on the hindquarters. When he does, rub him to let him know that's what you wanted. Tap him again and have him go past you.

Go back to the trailer and more circling. When your horse wants to rest, let it be at the trailer door. Apply the go-past cue as your horse puts his front feet in the trailer. He might walk his hind feet up to the floor and get stalled out, but recognize that as a try.

Keep tapping and eventually he'll stick all four feet in the trailer. If he needs to come back out again, let him. Don't make a fuss and don't slam shut the door. Let him know he can come out under his own steam and everything's okay.

Rub him, then put him back to work circling again. The resting spot in the beginning is at the trailer door, but by the time you're done, it'll be all the way inside the trailer.

In any trailer-loading session, load your horse 15 or 20 times to cement the idea in his mind. Some horses are fine loading for three or four times, then they quit. It's like a role reversal. The horse thinks he's in charge and decides to not try anymore. So you need to make an indelible impression on your horse, one he won't soon forget.

## Unload Your Horse

Your horse should learn how to unload at the time you teach him to load. It's possible that he won't know how to back out of a trailer, so make sure you've taught your horse to back before you put him inside any trailer. Use the backing exercises in Chapter 12 to help you with this.

If the trailer is big enough inside, go in with your horse. Rub and reassure him that things are okay. Then ask him to back out of the trailer one step at a time. Bump his halter rope or press on his chest with your fingertips or swagger stick and say "back, back, back." He should know this from earlier lessons. As your horse backs, don't keep pushing on him. Let him do the work on his own. Help him only as needed.

If the trailer isn't big enough, such as an inline trailer or a two-horse, use your lead rope to bump your horse out, using the same verbal backing cues.

However, as mentioned above, when your horse backs out of a trailer on his own, he's in effect teaching himself to unload, so don't discourage horses that put one or two feet in, then immediately back out.

Some horses develop the bad habit of backing out of a trailer too quickly. Like most bad habits, it's easy to make and hard to break.

Have a trailer-loading session specifically to deal with this problem. Load your horse in the trailer and if he wants to run out, let him, but put him right back in. Do this repeatedly, making the wrong thing difficult and the right thing easy. You can even circle him outside the trailer, just as you did in trailer training. Put him to work. The resting spot now is in the trailer.

Soon, your horse will slow down. He'll put effort into unloading slowly. Instead of coming out so quickly, eventually he'll wait for you to ask him to step out of the trailer.

## Problem Loaders

If you have a problem trailer-loading horse, the last place you should go is the trailer. You already know your horse won't load. Why bother? That would be making an issue and a fight out of the trailer.

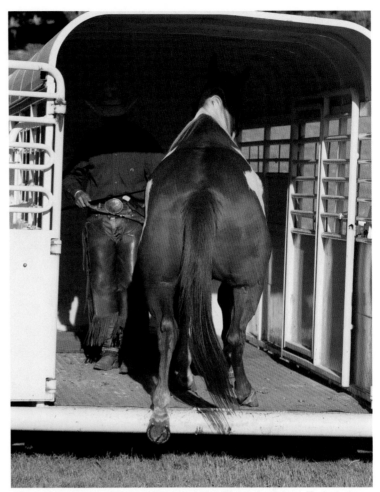

*Allow the horse to back out at any time, then reload him. To help him back out, tap his chest with the swagger stick.*

# A BETTER WAY

### Bad Haulers

Some horses are just bad haulers. Possibly they were the victims of bad drivers, who stopped and started too quickly, throwing the animals all over the trailer when they did. But for whatever reason, now the horse paws, scrambles or kicks repeatedly in the trailer. It's a nuisance to the driver and potentially harmful to the horse.

Try putting the horse in a different position in the trailer to see if that stops his behavior. Or allow him to stand backward. Depending on your trailer and the circumstances, this might not be viable. Also, you might try hauling him with a friend or buddy, which sometimes has a calming effect on a bad hauler.

I'm not opposed to hobbling a bad hauler. I use my training hobbles, made of big, soft, cotton braids. Of course, I hobble-break the horse before I put him in the trailer. (See Chapter 11, "Hobble-Breaking.")

If the horse is a scrambler or kicker, I side-line hobble him right in the trailer. A side-line goes from one front leg to the corresponding hind leg and basically helps prevent the horse from scrambling. Standing still becomes the horse's best choice.

*Start over again, with more circles if you need to, then ask your horse to load again.*

## True Story: Freight-Training

*At one time I worked as a cowboy on the Ralph Lauren Double R Ranch in Ridgway, Colo. One fall day, a norther' blew in unexpectedly, bringing with it lots of wind and snow. The cowboys I worked with decided to load the horses and make a run for the headquarters.*

*With six horses all saddled and a big stock trailer, we began loading the horses one after the other. The last horse, a big bay, refused to load. The cowboys, cold and ready to go home, were in a hurry and had no interest in any "fine" trailer-loading techniques.*

*I took the initiative to step in the trailer, holding the balky horse's lead rope. The other cowboys hoo-rayed, whipped and tried to spook the horse into loading. The confused bay finally took a huge leap into the trailer and freight-trained headlong into me. I escaped, but not without a laceration and a broken nose. This is a good example of how not to load your horse.*

*The key to correct trailer loading is preparation and patience, which translates into confidence in the horse. There's nothing better than a horse that loads and unloads on command.*

Your horse needs fundamentals in forward movement (See Chapter 9, "Ground Work, the Foundation.") and longeing (See Chapter 12, "Longe-Line Techniques.") Do all those exercises first, so you'll have a chance. Develop a language between you and your horse before you ask him to load.

The whole idea is to prepare your horse, to make your idea become his idea. Then, he loads not because you make him, but because he wants to.

Try not to let your horse become hot during the sessions. A hot horse becomes angry and then doesn't think. This is especially true in hot, humid climates. If you see your horse becoming too hot, stop the session and cool or hose him off. With a truly angry horse, you might have to slow the process down and even stop to let him gain control over his emotions. Start again when he's calmer.

Trailer loading is a game of patience. Frustration or anger won't help you either; they only get in your way.

A true trailer-loading horse is a horse that can load with or without a halter, in rain or shine, sleet or snow, day or night. Great trailer loading is an ultimate expression of trust and confidence.

*When he can load repeatedly without much urging from you, your horse is broke to trailer loading.*

# HERE'S HOW

## Trailering Tips

Give your horse a good experience in the trailer and he won't mind hopping in it for you. His comfort is all-important as you haul him down the road. Here are some tips for traveling.

- **Ventilation** — Horses are more hot-natured than humans and would prefer to be a little cool, rather than too hot. They generate lots of heat in an enclosed trailer. Make sure your trailer is properly ventilated. Open the drop-down windows, if you have them, to let in fresh air, even in cool weather.

- **Footing** — Put shavings down on the floorboards. That helps with road heat and noise. Also, it's a cushion between your horse's feet and the hard floorboards.

- **Rest Stops** — Unload horses every 4 or 5 hours. Dealing with road vibration is a lot of work for a horse; allow him to rest and relax for a few minutes outside the trailer. Many rest stops even have grassy areas, so let your horse graze a little. These short breaks are great for his mind.

- **Water** — Offer water at every opportunity. Many horses won't drink well on the road, but try to water them anyway. Carry a watering container and bucket and offer your horse water at rest and fueling stops.

- **Blankets** — If it's extremely cold, consider blanketing or sheeting your horse. A lot depends on your trailer. If it's a stock trailer, the wind could howl through the slats and, if you're traveling 65 miles an hour, a blanket might feel good to your horse. But in a totally enclosed trailer, he might do just fine in his own skin.

- **Tying** — Don't tie too high or too long. You don't want your horse to get his foot over the rope, but make sure your length of rope allows him to lower his head to a comfortable level. Most horses like to lower their heads to blow accumulated dust out their noses. In a slant-load or side-by-side trailer, you don't have to tie experienced travelers at all. It's best to tie novice haulers, though, so they don't cause any trouble.

*Trailers with drop-down windows provide ventilation for horses.*

# CONCLUSION

I hope you enjoyed reading this book as much as I did writing it. On its pages I've tried to give you a solid foundation in all aspects of horsemanship, from understanding equine psychology to equitation basics, and from colt-starting fundamentals to high-performance training techniques. Plus, along the way, I've provided solutions to common riding and horse-management problems. Remember: Knowledge is a treasure, but practice is the key and experience the best teacher. Don't be afraid of making mistakes when you try any of the methods or exercises offered in this book. Just be sure to learn from them. Bear in mind that your horse is also learning.

Your ultimate goal as a good horseman is to have your horse become a willing partner who performs through understanding and not out of pain or fear. The best horsemen I know who accomplish this partnership are continually learning, challenging themselves and changing. If you can't change, you can't grow. And if you can't grow, you can't be your best. Work on your horsemanship with desire, determination and dedication. When you do, there's no limit to what you can achieve. *Ride smart!*

—*Craig Cameron*

# MY LIFE: CRAIG CAMERON

## *"Horses have been my life, and I'm still working at it."*

I always knew what I wanted to be — a cowboy — and I was fortunate because my family has always been involved in the ranching business. I was born in 1949 to Bruce and Frances Cameron. My dad was an orthopedic surgeon in Houston, Texas, but my grandparents, Ed and Sadie Gough, had a ranch in Cat Spring, Texas, great cow country with rolling hills dotted with live oak trees.

As a kid, I loved the land, the cattle and the wildlife, but mostly I loved the cowboys and the horses. I was always intrigued by the trappings of ranching and cowboy gear — the boots, spurs, saddles and tack. I loved being involved when it was time to work the cattle and being part of the everyday routine of ranch life.

I can remember going to the Houston Livestock Show and Rodeo and watching the rodeo cowboys closely. I knew right then and there that one day I would not only be a ranch cowboy, but a rodeo cowboy as well. In high school, I was very athletic and played football and ran track, but it was then that I also got involved in rodeo. When I went to Stephen F. Austin College, I studied animal science, but rodeoing and ranching kept calling me back.

When my grandfather died, we sold the ranch in Cat Spring and my grandmother bought the Hickory Creek Ranch in Giddings, Texas. We still own this ranch today. When I was in my early 20s, I ran the ranch and worked it as a cow-calf and stocker operation. While running the outfit for 15 years, I also rodeoed, won my Professional Rodeo Cowboys Association card and traveled all over the United States, Canada and Mexico. I broke a lot of bones — leg, arm, ribs and collarbone. I've punctured my lungs and had a knee operation. But no matter, I was truly a ranch and rodeo cowboy. I was living my childhood dream.

We all need inspiration in our lives, and I've been truly lucky to have had great men inspire me. One of the earliest influences in my life was a man by the name of C.P. Hamer, whose dad, brother and other family members were famous Texas Rangers. He was our foreman at both ranches, and he taught me the importance of hard work, honesty and the cowboy ethics that have stuck with me today: You work for your pay, and your handshake and word are your bond. I did a lot of cowboying with him. He taught me how to ranch and how to stretch a dollar. He showed me the ins and outs of the cattle business.

However, it was the horses that interested me the most. I've always had a "thing" for horses even as a little kid. I like the way they sound, the way they move and even the way they smell. I still do.

As I look back I realize how old-fashioned things really were then, including the handling of horses. Although there have always been great horsemen — men ahead of their time, such as Monte Foreman, Dale Wilkinson, Jimmy Williams and Tom and Bill Dorrance — the more common approach to horsemanship back then was more of a "show 'em who's the boss and make 'em do it" attitude. It wasn't about teaching the horse; it was more about force, pain and bigger bits. Always, in my soul, I knew there was a better way.

I've been laughed at many times and put down for trying to take a slower, gentler approach in the training of horses. But at that time there were no clinicians or clinics to attend. Truthfully, I had no teacher. It was truly the school of hard knocks for me and there were plenty of them because I had an abundance of tough and abused horses to deal with.

Craig making an 81-point ride in the open pro finals,
Fredericksburg, Texas, 1985.

Remember that, at that time, just being a cowboy was pretty darn tough. It was a time of hip, cool and a new sensation called the Beatles. More than once I had to literally fight just because I wore a cowboy hat. I, like some of you, was cowboy when cowboy wasn't cool. But, I was determined and people who know me will tell you I have no "quit" in me. I ranched, rodeoed and kept trying to work horses, my style, the best I could. Then a change came.

During the late 1970s, a man named Hank Kershner from Oregon came to work with me at the ranch. We rode lots of horses together, and he told me that I needed to meet Ray Hunt and see how he worked horses.

Around 1980, I had the opportunity to watch Ray at a clinic in San Angelo, Texas. It was the turning point in my life. I watched him work with horses, not against them. He emphasized the need to understand the nature of the horse. He stressed giving the horse a chance to learn. He said, "Give 'em time." He spoke about

thinking like a horse and putting yourself in the horse's place. Work on yourself, he said, and not so much on the horse. This man inspired me and changed my life.

I went back to the ranch determined to become a better horseman. I worked with any horse that was brought me — old horses, young horses and any breed. It didn't matter; they were all horses. The horse became my teacher. I developed my own style and techniques, but always with the idea of working through understanding with the horse.

Folks would bring me their really tough horses, and when they would see remarkable results, they'd want to come and watch. They wanted to know what I was doing. Finally, I began making them pay for the privilege and when I did, they really started listening.

I had my first clinic at my family's Hickory Creek Ranch in the mid-1980s. People brought me a lot of mustangs to ride, and they were amazed at what I got accomplished. Slowly, but surely, I started traveling and demonstrating my techniques of working through understanding with horses, first, in Texas, then nationwide. Without checking or screening, I would take on any horse. The demonstrations included colt breaking, problem solving, trailer loading, reining and the philosophy of horsemanship.

Take my word for it, these demonstrations got pretty western a lot of times. In the beginning, people didn't come to learn as much as they came to see me fail. Humans are born skeptics and I was in a business that brought out skepticism in a big way. Often, an old-timer would just not believe. I would ask him to bring me his horse. Sure enough, he would get up, leave and come back an hour later with a horse in tow in some old stock trailer. I always say it's a bad sign when they have to back the trailer up to the round pen to get the horse into it.

Amazingly, horses never let me down. Working through patience and understanding, I've always been able to have them make incredible progress. Those old-timers would stick out their hands to me and say, "I'm a believer now."

Over the years, I've had other believers. I've been connected with lots of celebrities who had me ride their horses — Buck Taylor, Lynn Anderson, Ralph Lauren, Bum Phillips, Red Steagall and others.

Famed Quarter Horse breeder L.A. Waters, who owned the legendary cutting-horse sire Colonel Freckles, hired me to train his horses at his Fulshear, Texas, ranch. He had watched me at a clinic and kept after me to work for him. He finally made me an offer I couldn't refuse. I held clinics at the ranch every month. They became so successful we didn't have to advertise. People would just show up the first Saturday of every month.

After Waters dispersed his operation, I went to Bobby Hunt's cutting-horse training facility in Simonton, Texas. I worked at his ranch for several years, taking in outside horses and putting on clinics. It was there that I began specializing in 1-hour demonstrations, where I'd ride any horse people brought me. Around this time, I got hired by cowboy singer Michael Martin Murphey to work his WestFests for a number of years. There are many annual events that I've been repeating for 10 years and the crowds just keep getting bigger.

I've also put on clinics at famous Texas cattle ranches, such as the Pitchfork and JA, both historical ranching operations. I'm proud to think that I've helped their cowboys try to better their horses and their horsemanship. Now if that's not the ultimate dream of a kid who always wanted to be a cowboy, I don't know what is.

It's now 20 years later and I am still at it. I've become a modern-day traveling cowboy. The only open range left today is the highway. Traveling worldwide, starting thousands of horses and meeting thousands of horse people have been my privilege and my life. Through it all, whether by myself, or working in front of a huge crowd at a modern horse expo, when tempted to shortcut or lose my cool, I always visualize Ray Hunt sitting on the round-pen fence watching me. This keeps me right and keeps me correct. I thank him as I know the horse does.

I met my wife, Dalene, during the filming of a cowboy documentary on a ranch in Weatherford, Texas, in the early 1990s. I worked as a wrangler and extra on the film and Dalene happened to be there with some friends who were involved with the production. A beautiful girl, Dalene really caught my eye, and we began a steady relationship for several years and later married. We purchased the Double Horn Ranch in Bluff Dale, Texas, together and developed it for our clinics and seminars. A cutting-horse rider, Dalene's got a great way with a horse, is one of the better riders I've ever seen and has taught me a lot. A relentless worker, Dalene is the driving force behind Craig Cameron Horsemanship.

I've been called the Cowboy's Clinician. I'd like to think I've made a lot of good changes for a lot of horses and hopefully a lot of people, too. Horses have been my life and I'm still working at it.

*Dalene and Craig on the Double Horn Ranch, Bluff Dale, Texas.*

# WHAT THEY SAY ABOUT THE COWBOY'S CLINICIAN

Since you've picked up this book, we probably share a common passion — a love of horses. I've loved horses my whole life. I think they're perfect animals, and I've spent my entire life on their backs. Since I've retired from rough-stock riding, I've had more time to pursue my goal of becoming a better horseman. I've also been lucky enough to live just 15 minutes away from a world-class hand — Craig Cameron.

I met Craig 10 years ago while we were both working cows on a north Texas ranch. There are several things that impressed me about Craig then, and they still do today. He has a genuine love and compassion for horses. He respects them enough to try to see things through their eyes. It's amazing to see how much a horse will give you when you work from an understanding of how the horse perceives and experiences the world around him. Craig always tries to better understand a horse's point of view so he can communicate with him in a way he easily understands. No fighting or confusion.

Another of Craig's great traits: As masterful and adept as Craig is at his craft, he's always open to learning more. He doesn't have a big ego that's fooled him into believing he's "arrived" at a training formula. This is a valuable quality to possess if you want to be great at anything.

Not only is Craig a great horseman, he's also great at teaching people to become horsemen, which is an art in itself.

I've really enjoyed all the time I've spent with Craig, and all he's shared with me. He's one "helluva" cowboy and an even better person.

If you want to learn how to better communicate with your horse, then you'll love this book.

—*Ty Murray*
*Seven-time World Champion All-Around PRCA Cowboy*

Craig has been the biggest influence in our lives in learning the true meaning of understanding and communicating with the horse. He's a master at it.

—*Butch & Joy Murray*
*Ty Murray's parents*

Craig asked me to participate in the Top Gun clinic at his Double Horn Ranch in Bluff Dale, Texas, and for it he'd invited horsemen from various disciplines and equine sports to put on demonstrations. I put on cutting and reining demos. Craig was as much into what I was doing as I was into what he did. Good horsemen always want to continue to learn and share both.

I was so impressed with his presentation as a clinician and noticed how the spectators were enthralled with whatever he had to say. Craig has a lot of charisma, and it's obvious by watching the people watch him work.

Craig put on a colt-starting demonstration. I mean this was a real bronc, and it broke in two when Craig put the saddle on it for the first time. I was fascinated as he explained his philosophy about horses and how they think and feel. It was a true horseman's insight. In a short time, he rode the bronc. He didn't have to run it out of air or wear it down either. He didn't "steal" a ride, as they say. He had the "feel" to do it with intuition. Craig got to be part of the horse, and the horse trusted him. It was a great experience for me to be there.

Since then, we've worked together on other clinics. I have a high degree of respect for Craig, his expertise and the way he can read a horse's mind. He truly enjoys what he does.

But, besides all that, he's a danged good guy and fun to be around. It's good to call him my friend.

—*Al Dunning*
*Multiple world champion reiner, cutter and reined cow-horse rider*

Craig's genuinely friendly and caring personality works magic with all types of people from beginning riders to the working cowboy. He helps folks to help the horse and the horse to help folks.

—*James Gholson*
*Wagon Boss, Pitchfork Ranch*

I'm pleased my friend Craig Cameron has chosen to share his gift of knowledge with us through this book. There are many horsemen who communicate well with horses, but most lack the ability to communicate with other people. Craig has the ability to communicate with both the knowledgeable horseman as well as the most novice horse enthusiast.

Craig embodies the western way of life and has helped keep our western heritage alive. He's a straight shooter — what he demonstrates in town, he practices on his ranches. Humility and frankness go a long way with horses and people.

*—Mark Chestnut*
*Trainer and breeder*
*of NCHA and AQHA champions*

I'm extremely impressed with Craig Cameron's style and smooth hands when it comes to teaching young horses what their lives are all about. His soft approach and delivery were without question successfully disseminated to all our young ranch colts in an extraordinarily short period of time. I've adopted many of his practices and gentleness in my own style with great results, and I'm getting much stronger performance from our horses.

*—John Anderson*
*Manager, JA Ranch, Colorado*

Throughout my 25 years in the horse industry, I've found Craig Cameron to be one of the finest horsemen I've had the pleasure to be associated with. Craig's true love of horses, patience, kind hand and many years of problem-solving experience have produced great results with my horses.

We've worked together at my clinics and he offers an exciting new element for my students.

I think each person who reads this book will find that Craig's ideas and exercises better their horsemanship and understanding of the horse.

*—Charmayne James*
*11-time PRCA Barrel Racing World Champion*

Craig Cameron is a cowboy's trainer. He trains cowboys to train horses correctly. He makes it simple for us simple cowboys. We've learned how to do it an easier way than we did, thanks to Craig.

*—Bob Moorhouse*
*Vice president and manager*
*Pitchfork Land and Cattle Co.*

Craig Cameron: Capable, Common Sense and Charisma. He has charisma, which draws people, common sense (horse sense), which you can learn to use on horses as well as people, and years of experience, which have proven his capability.

*—Bruce McShan*
*Owner, McShan Ranch, Red River, N.M.*

Craig and I became friends when we were just teenage bull riders. After that gig was over, we were young cattle ranchers. Our ranches were close together, so, on occasion, Craig would help us with our cattle work. I still think about one incident that probably helped transform Craig Cameron into the horseman he is today. As a joke, during one of our roundups, I had a horse picked for Craig that was, without a doubt, the worst spoiled bronc that ever showed up on our place. This horse knew no forward, only reverse with a few spins in the middle. We didn't get much work done that day, for trying to ride our own horses and laughing at Craig in high speed reverse. We were all amazed that he never gave up on the outlaw for the entire day. Near the end, the bronc was actually taking some forward steps. Craig vowed from that day forward that no horse like that would ever exist if he could help it. Thanks to Craig and his methods, he's keeping his promise.

*—Bobby Steiner*
*1973 World Champion Bull Rider*

# CRAIG CAMERON'S COWBOY LOGIC

## Words of wisdom for the horse-wise.

- Smart riding is making sure you can ride tomorrow.
- Deposit your ego before you enter the corral.
- If you don't remember anything else, remember to go slowly.
- Your goal is to make the horse more relaxed than when you started.
- The horse seeks the level of the rider.
- A good horseman knows when to quit.
- Don't forget the resting spot; that's where the horse relaxes and becomes gentle.
- To control the hindquarters is to control the horse's engine.
- Great horsemanship takes time.
- Correction is good, but encouragement is better.
- Hindsight is 20/20. Foresight is priceless.
- Patience is waiting without worry.
- Experience can sometimes be a tough teacher.
- I've never seen a horse that was too tired to buck.
- A good horse is like a good man. Turn him loose, and let him work.
- No man stands taller than when he sits on the back of a horse.
- If you can't change, then you can't grow. If you can't grow, then you can't be your best.
- Habit - easiest thing to make, hardest to break.
- Green on green makes black and blue.
- The way you ride today constitutes the kind of horse you'll ride tomorrow.
- If a horse is scared, get off and show him the way. That's part of making a horse strong where he's weak and brave when he's afraid.

# PROFILE: KATHY SWAN

Kathy Swan considers herself one of the lucky ones to be able to combine her passions for reading, writing and riding into her life's work.

A lifelong horsewoman, Kathy has explored many trails. She's earned local, regional and national awards in both American Quarter Horse Association and American Paint Horse Association competition, in a variety of English and western classes. She's also competed successfully in North American Trail Conference rides and in hunter trials. Breeding Quarter Horses and Paints had been a serious hobby of hers for years, but she's also owned Arabians, Thoroughbreds and Andalusians. Today, she's an avid trail rider and enjoys seeing the West horseback.

Kathy has won awards for both her writing and her photography. She has a broad background in the equine publication industry: news editor at the *Quarter Horse News*, editor of *Horseman* and *Horse & Rider* magazines, and associate editor at *Western Horseman*. Currently, she's the editor of *Equestrian Retailer* magazine and the *Western Horseman* book division.

Other titles by the writer (under her former name, Kadash) include two best sellers: *Reining, the Art of Performance in Horses* by Bob Loomis and *Natural Horse-Man-Ship* by Pat Parelli.

**Kathy Swan and Craig Cameron.**

# Books Published by
# WESTERN HORSEMAN®

**ARABIAN LEGENDS** by Marian K. Carpenter
280 pages and 319 photographs. Abu Farwa, *Aladdinn, *Ansata Ibn Halima, *Bask, Bay-Abi, Bay El Bey, Bint Sahara, Fadjur, Ferzon, Indraff, Khemosabi, *Morafic, *Muscat, *Naborr, *Padron, *Raffles, *Raseyn, *Sakr, Samtyr, *Sanacht, *Serafix, Skorage, *Witez II, Xenophonn.

**BACON & BEANS** by Stella Hughes
144 pages and 200-plus recipes. Try the best in western chow.

**CALF ROPING** by Roy Cooper
144 pages and 280 photographs. Complete coverage of roping and tying.

**CUTTING** by Leon Harrel
144 pages and 200 photographs. Complete guide to this popular sport.

**FIRST HORSE** by Fran Devereux Smith
176 pages, 160 black-and-white photos, numerous illustrations. Step-by-step information for the first-time horse owner and/or novice rider.

**HELPFUL HINTS FOR HORSEMEN**
128 pages and 325 photographs and illustrations. WH readers and editors provide tips on every facet of life with horses and offer solutions to common problems horse owners share. Chapters include: Equine Health Care; Saddles; Bits and Bridles; Gear; Knots; Trailers/Hauling Horses; Trail Riding/Backcountry Camping; Barn Equipment; Watering Systems; Pasture, Corral and Arena Equipment; Fencing and Gates; Odds and Ends.

**IMPRINT TRAINING** by Robert M. Miller, D.V.M.
144 pages and 250 photographs. Learn to "program" newborn foals.

**LEGENDS 1** by Diane Ciarloni
168 pages and 214 photographs. Barbra B, Bert, Chicaro Bill, Cowboy P-12, Depth Charge (TB), Doc Bar, Go Man Go, Hard Twist, Hollywood Gold, Joe Hancock, Joe Reed P-3, Joe Reed II, King P-234, King Fritz, Leo, Peppy, Plaudit, Poco Bueno, Poco Tivio, Queenie, Quick M Silver, Shue Fly, Star Duster, Three Bars (TB), Top Deck (TB) and Wimpy P-1.

**LEGENDS 2** by Jim Goodhue, Frank Holmes, Phil Livingston, Diane Ciarloni
192 pages and 224 photographs. Clabber, Driftwood, Easy Jet, Grey Badger II, Jessie James, Jet Deck, Joe Bailey P-4 (Gonzales), Joe Bailey (Weatherford), King's Pistol, Lena's Bar, Lightning Bar, Lucky Blanton, Midnight, Midnight Jr, Moon Deck, My Texas Dandy, Oklahoma Star, Oklahoma Star Jr., Peter McCue, Rocket Bar (TB), Skipper W, Sugar Bars and Traveler.

**LEGENDS 3** by Jim Goodhue, Frank Holmes, Diane Ciarloni, Kim Guenther, Larry Thornton, Betsy Lynch
208 pages and 196 photographs. Flying Bob, Hollywood Jac 86, Jackstraw (TB), Maddon's Bright Eyes, Mr Gun Smoke, Old Sorrel, Piggin String (TB), Poco Lena, Poco Pine, Poco Dell, Question Mark, Quo Vadis, Royal King, Showdown, Steel Dust and Two Eyed Jack.

**LEGENDS 4**
216 pages and 216 photographs. Several authors chronicle the great Quarter Horses Zantanon, Ed Echols, Zan Parr Bar, Blondy's Dude, Diamonds Sparkle, Woven Web/Miss Princess, Miss Bank, Rebel Cause, Tonto Bars Hank, Harlan, Lady Bug's Moon, Dash For Cash, Vandy, Impressive, Fillinic, Zippo Pine Bar and Doc O' Lena.

**LEGENDS 5** by Frank Holmes, Ty Wyant, Alan Gold, Sally Harrison
248 pages, including about 300 photographs. The stories of Little Joe, Joe Moore, Monita, Bill Cody, Joe Cody, Topsail Cody, Pretty Buck, Pat Star Jr., Skipa Star, Hank H, Chubby, Bartender, Leo San, Custus Rastus (TB), Jaguar, Jackie Bee, Chicado V and Mr Bar None.

**LEGENDS 6** by Frank Holmes, Patricia Campbell, Sally Harrison, Glory Ann Kurtz, Cheryl Magoteaux, Heidi Nyland, Bev Pechan, Juli S. Thorson
236 pages, including about 270 photographs. The stories of Paul A, Croton Oil, Okie Leo Flit Bar, Billietta, Coy's Bonanza, Major Bonanza, Doc Quixote, Doc's Prescription, Jewels Leo Bar, Colonel Freckles, Freckles Playboy, Peppy San, Mr San Peppy, Great Pine, The Invester, Speedy Glow, Conclusive, Dynamic Deluxe and Caseys Charm

**NATURAL HORSE-MAN-SHIP** by Pat Parelli
224 pages and 275 photographs. Parelli's six keys to a natural horse-human relationship.

**PROBLEM-SOLVING, Volume 1** by Marty Marten
248 pages and over 250 photos and illustrations. Develop a willing partnership between horse and human — trailer-loading, hard-to-catch, barn-sour, spooking, water-crossing, herd-bound and pull-back problems.

**PROBLEM-SOLVING, Volume 2** by Marty Marten
A continuation of Volume 1. Ten chapters with illustrations and photos.

**RAISE YOUR HAND IF YOU LOVE HORSES** by Pat Parelli w. Kathy Swan
224 pages and over 200 black and white and color photos. The autobiography of the world's foremost proponent of natural horsemanship. Chapters contain hundreds of Pat Parelli stories, from the clinician's earliest remembrances to the fabulous experiences and opportunities he has enjoyed in the last decade. As a bonus, there are anecdotes in which Pat's friends tell stories about him.

**RANCH HORSEMANSHIP** by Curt Pate w. Fran Devereux Smith
220 pages and over 250 full color photos and illustrations. Learn how almost any rider at almost any level of expertise can adapt ranch-horse-training techniques to help his mount become a safer more enjoyable ride. Curt's ideas help prepare rider and horse for whatever they might encounter in the round pen, arena, pasture and beyond.

**REINING, Completely Revised** by Al Dunning
216 pages and over 300 photographs. Complete how-to training for this exciting event.

**RIDE SMART,** by Craig Cameron w. Kathy Swan
224 pages and over 250 black and white and color photos. Under one title, Craig Cameron combines a look at horses as a species and how to develop a positive, partnering relationship with them, along with good, solid horsemanship skills that suit both novice and experienced riders. Topics include ground-handling techniques, hobble-breaking methods, colt-starting, high performance maneuvers and trailer-loading. Interesting sidebars, such as trouble-shooting tips and personal anecdotes about Cameron's life, complement the main text.

**RODEO LEGENDS** by Gavin Ehringer
Photos and life stories fill 216 pages. Included are: Joe Alexander, Jake Barnes & Clay O'Brien Cooper, Joe Beaver, Leo Camarillo, Roy Cooper, Tom Ferguson, Bruce Ford, Marvin Garrett, Don Gay, Tuff Hedeman, Charmayne James, Bill Linderman, Larry Mahan, Ty Murray, Dean Oliver, Jim Shoulders, Casey Tibbs, Harry Tompkins and Fred Whitfield.

**ROOFS AND RAILS** by Gavin Ehringer
144 pages, 128 black-and-white photographs plus drawings, charts and floor plans. How to plan and build your ideal horse facility.

**STARTING COLTS** by Mike Kevil
168 pages and 400 photographs. Step-by-step process in starting colts.

**THE HANK WIESCAMP STORY** by Frank Holmes
208 pages and over 260 photographs. The biography of the legendary breeder of Quarter Horses, Appaloosas and Paints.

**TEAM PENNING** by Phil Livingston
144 pages and 200 photographs. How to compete in this popular family sport.

**TEAM ROPING WITH JAKE AND CLAY** by Fran Devereux Smith
224 pages and over 200 photographs and illustrations. Learn about fast times from champions Jake Barnes and Clay O'Brien Cooper. Solid information about handling a rope, roping dummies and heading and heeling for practice and in competition. Also sound advice about rope horses, roping steers, gear and horsemanship.

**WELL-SHOD** by Don Baskins
160 pages, 300 black-and-white photos and illustrations. A horse-shoeing guide for owners and farriers. Easy-to-read, step-by-step how to trim and shoe a horse for a variety of uses. Special attention is paid to corrective shoeing for horses with various foot and leg problems.

**WESTERN TRAINING** by Jack Brainard
With Peter Phinny. 136 pages. Stresses the foundation for western training.

**WIN WITH BOB AVILA** by Juli S. Thorson
Hardbound, 128 full-color pages. Learn the traits that separate horse-world achievers from also-rans. World champion horseman Bob Avila shares his philosophies on succeeding as a competitor, breeder and trainer.

Western Horseman, established in 1936, is the world's leading horse publication. For subscription information: 800-877-5278.
To order other Western Horseman books: 800-874-6774 • Western Horseman, Box 7980, Colorado Springs, CO 80933-7980.
Web site: **www.westernhorseman.com**.